SPOTLIGHT

Solo Scenes for Student Actors

STEPHANIE S. FAIRBANKS

MERIWETHER PUBLISHING LTD
Colorado Springs, Colorado

Meriwether Publishing Ltd., Publisher
P.O. Box 7710
Colorado Springs, CO 80933

Editor: Theodore O. Zapel
Typesetting: Sharon E. Garlock
Cover design: Tom Myers

© Copyright MCMXCVI Meriwether Publishing Ltd.
Printed in the United States of America
First Edition

Library of Congress Cataloging-in-Publication Data

Fairbanks, Stephanie, 1950-
        Spotlight : solo scenes for student actors / by Stephanie
Fairbanks -- 1st ed.
            p.   cm.
        ISBN 1-56608-020-7 (pbk.)
        1. Acting. 2. Monologues.   I. Title.
    PN2080.F35   1996
 𝑌𝐴 812'.54--dc20   96-6169
                                                                            CIP
                                                                            AC

1   2   3   4   5   6   7   8   99   98   97   96

for
Greg, Aunt Thomza
and the Strobels,
Dallas, Hunter, Gus
William & Mary Morgan

Contents

Introduction

Spotlight is the result of an acting workshop I directed in a program for gifted students in Pensacola, Florida. Writing the scenes came first out of necessity, but seeing my own characters come to life on stage motivated me to continue writing.

Some of these characters you will recognize from stories you've heard before, but most have evolved from the experiences of the students I have taught and counseled over the years. These are situations young actors can easily understand and project to the audience. All of the scenes can be staged with a minimum of props and a few simple costumes.

EDITOR'S NOTE: Many of the monologs in this book use props and costumes to set the scene and enhance each characterization. Most of the costumes and props are optional and many are shown in pantomime. All of the suggested props are described at the opening of each monolog for your ease in preparing for performance.

The numerals running vertically down the left margin of each page of dialog are for the convenience of the director. With these, he/she may easily direct attention to a specific passage.

Part One:

MONOLOGS FOR GIRLS

1. Call Waiting

1   *(GIRL enters carrying phone. NOTE: A ringing sound effect*
2   *is required.)* **Oh, he is *so* cool.** *(Staring at the phone)* **Call me,**
3   **Andrew. *Please,* call me. He looked at us today. No, he stared.**
4   **Jenny and I were sitting two tables across from him at lunch,**
5   **and every time I looked up, he was smiling. He has the most**
6   **gorgeous blue eyes. Maybe he wants to ask me to the**
7   **Valentine's Dance. Maybe I'll ask him...** *(Starts to pick up the*
8   *phone.)* **No. I can't. Maybe I'll get Jenny to ask him for me.**
9   *(Phone rings and she hesitates then composes herself.)* **Please,**
10   **let it be him!** *(Picks up phone.)* **Oh, Jenny, it's you. Yeah, I was**
11   **just thinking about you, too. Actually, I was thinking about the**
12   **dance. What...Andrew? Yeah, that's what I was going to talk to**
13   **you about...What...You want *me* to call him...for *you*?** *(Pause)*
14   **Sure, I'm your best friend, but...** *(Pause)* **you want me to say**
15   **you're thinking about what?** *(Frantically)* **Jenny, you can't ask**
16   **Andrew to the dance...Well...because...girls don't ask guys to**
17   **dances! Besides he may be going with somebody else.** *(Pause)*
18   **Who? I don't know who. What do you think I am...a mind**
19   **reader?** *(Pause)* **No, I'm not upset. Why would I be upset? You**
20   **want to go to the dance with Andrew Baker, you call him**
21   **yourself. Listen, I'm really busy right now. Did you get those**
22   **problems in math? Hey, Jen, hold on a minute, I've got**
23   **somebody on the other line...**
24   **Hello...** *(Her mood brightens.)* **Andrew...** *(Giggles.)* **Oh,**
25   **nothing much. What've you been doing? Yeah, I saw you at**
26   **lunch today. You should've come over. What?** *(Pause)*
27   **Valentine's Dance...** *(Giggles.)* **Yeah, I've been thinking I might**
28   **go.** *(Pause)* **Jen? Does she have a date? Well, I don't know,**
29   **Andrew. I don't keep up with her social calendar.** *(Getting*
30   *more irritated)* **What? Would I mind asking her if she wants to**
31   **go with you?** *(Looks at the phone.)* **What is this anyway**
32   **...Western Union? Ask her yourself!** *(Presses call waiting button.)*

1   *(Impatiently)* **Jen...I gotta go now. No...wrong number,**
2   **that's all. And, Jen,** *(Pause)* **don't call me back tonight, no**
3   **matter how happy you are.** *(Pause)* **Oh, you'll get it, all right! In**
4   **about five minutes. And when you do, I** *don't* **want to hear**
5   **about it! And, Jen...if I don't speak to you tomorrow, don't take**
6   **it personally.** *(Slams phone down and exits.)*
7
8
9
10
11
12
13
14
15
16
17
18
19
20
21
22
23
24
25
26
27
28
29
30
31
32
33
34
35

2. Wallflower

1   *(GIRL enters wearing green party dress.)* **Ar-r-rg! I feel like**
2 **an umbrella. I hate this green dress! Why does it have to stick**
3 **straight out?** *(Motions to others around her.)* **Excuse me, please.**
4 **Could you make a little space...for my dress? Yes, thanks...a**
5 **little** *wall* **space. I have to stand. I couldn't sit if I wanted to.**
6 **Maybe I ought to sit. That corner would be nice. But nobody**
7 **would ask me to dance then. There's a rule somewhere that**
8 **says: If you want to dance, you have to stand along the wall.**
9 **Sure, I've been standing here forty-five minutes and still**
10 **nobody asks me to dance...except Melinda, and if we get out**
11 **there no one will ask us to dance — boys, I mean. Another rule:**
12 **Girls do not dance with girls.**

13   **Oh, I hate dances and I hate boys, too, for that matter! It's**
14 **not fair. Boys get to make all the decisions and girls just have**
15 **to stand around and wait. Like now, for instance. Here I stand**
16 **like a big green frog till some guy casually strolls over here to**
17 **ask me for a dance. I mean, I have to** *wait* **to be chosen. I hate**
18 **that!**

19   **How should I stand? Like this?** *(Poses slumped over with*
20 *arms to her sides.)* **No, I look like a baby gorilla with my**
21 **knuckles dragging the floor. How about this?** *(She poses again.)*
22 **Hand on hip, weight shifted to the right, casual, laid back...No,**
23 **that's not me.**

24   **This is me.** *(Stands pigeon-toed with finger in mouth.)*
25 **Duh...'scuze me, Harold. Would you please ask me to dance?**
26 **I'll give you my lunch money. Oh, I hate being a wallflower. I**
27 **hate standing here on display and I hate the chaperons who**
28 **look at kids and whisper to each other and laugh. Oh...why am**
29 **I here anyway? What did I think would happen? Boy, am I**
30 **stupid. Stupid, stupid, stupid! Where is Jess? She said she'd be**
31 **here. At least then I'd have someone to talk to instead of just**
32 **sitting here like a goon.**

1   I'm taller than any guy here. Well, almost. There's Roger.
2   He's about my size. He's about twice my size. But Roger
3   doesn't dance much. He just stands around the snack table till
4   all the little sandwiches are gone, mayonnaise on the sides of
5   his mouth, broccoli dip between his teeth.
6   Ar-r-rg! This is the last time I go to a school dance. I'd
7   rather be in front of a firing squad. *(Gets rigid, puts hand over*
8   *eyes.)* Blindfold, cigarette, please. Any words to the folks back
9   home? H-E-L-P! I hate this. That's it. I've had it. *(Walks over to*
10 *left.)* Roger Wayne Richmond, I believe they are playing our
11 song. What? *(Disgusted)* I don't know what song. The "Star
12 Spangled Banner," for all I care. The point is...do you want to
13 dance with me or not, Roger? *(Begins rambling.)* And *please*,
14 don't do me any favors. A simple "yes" or "no," not a
15 "probably" or "maybe later" or any other excuse. If you don't
16 want to dance with me, fine...but what? You *do* want to dance.
17 Why...why, thank you, Roger. I'd love to. Don't you just *love*
18 these dances?
19
20
21
22
23
24
25
26
27
28
29
30
31
32
33
34
35

3. If the Shoe Fits

1   *(At rise, OLD WOMAN is sweeping with broom or in*
2   *pantomime.)* **All right, I've had enough of this! Outta here...all**
3   **of you!** *(Looks to right.)* **Suzie, get your fingers out of your nose**
4   **and do something constructive!** *(Moves to left.)* **Jennifer, stop**
5   **hitting your sister!** *(Swats them with real or imaginary broom.)*
6   **Out! Out!**
7   *(Shakes fist.)* **Mother Goose, wherever you are, I'll get you**
8   **for this!** *(Speaks to audience.)* **It's not enough that I have to live**
9   **in a shoe. That I can deal with! It's these kids that are driving**
10 **me crazy. And to think I coulda been a corporate executive for**
11 **IBM...business lunches...expense accounts! All this I traded for**
12 **a broom and a shoe? A house in the suburbs, maybe.** *(Pause)* **I**
13 **think this Mother Goose person must have had it in for her**
14 **own mother.**
15 **So...let's get down to the real story here, and it ain't**
16 **Cinderella. Listen, girls, check the fine print before you sign**
17 **on the dotted line, and if you get promised a little flat on 43rd**
18 **Street, don't do it, I'm telling you. A condo on the beach**
19 **maybe. This is ridiculous! Who can live in a shoe? There must**
20 **be a mix-up here.**
21 *(Focuses right.)* **Charlie, get your foot off you brother's**
22 **face! I've got enough to worry about already. Braces...always**
23 **another set of braces.** *(Hands on hips)* **Kids...aye, ya gotta love**
24 **'em! Otherwise, why would you put up with this stuff, I'd like**
25 **to know? Mother Goose, humph...**
26 *(Swats Downstage Left.)* **Jenna, get away from that TV set!**
27 **You want to get radiated?** *(Pauses to listen.)* **Looney Toons? Ha!**
28 **My life is a looney toon. Turn that thing off!**
29 *(Shakes fist again.)* **Mother Goose, I'll get you for this!**
30 *(Starts Off Right.)* **I know a duck that needs to be plucked.**
31
32

4. Old Mother Hubbard

1   *(A rocking chair is On-stage. OLD MOTHER HUBBARD*
2   *enters, calling the dog.)* **Here, Fido. Here, boy.** *(Whistles.)* **Come**
3   **on, poochie. Nice dog.** *(Pats his head.)* **Up, boy!** *(Pats her chest.)*
4   **Jump up, boy! Come on, Fido. Oh, well, lie down then if it**
5   **makes you feel better.** *(She sits slowly in the rocker.)* **We're not**
6   **as young as we used to be, are we, boy? Yeah, I know what you**
7   **mean. I've got a few gray hairs myself. Oh, my achin' bones.**
8   *(Pushes dog back.)* **No, not dog bones, you hungry mutt!** *Back*
9   **bones,** *leg* **bones,** *(Rubs neck)* *shoulder* **bones! It's been many a**
10   **winter we've sat here in front of this old fireplace, eh, Fido?**
11   **Why, I remember when you were just a pup. That time my**
12   **cupboard was bare and I couldn't find you a bone. That was**
13   **back in...** *(Long pause)* **Well, you were still wet behind the ears**
14   **and I was getting old, even then. Guess I've been old for lots**
15   **longer than I was young. Let me see now...next year I'll**
16   **be...well, never mind how old I'll be next year. What? You're**
17   **ninety-one in dog years? Why, Fido, you** *are* **an old codger.**
18   **Here I am a spry young thing. No advantage in being a dog, eh,**
19   **Fido?**
20   **He's good company, he is. Never complains or argues.**
21   **The old feller trips over his tongue to get to me every morning.**
22   **He's a good-natured dog with just one small fault...he snores!**
23   **There, do you hear him? He sounds like a buzz saw. Must be**
24   **dreaming he's out in the field somewhere chasing birds. Easy,**
25   **boy.** *(Pats him.)* **Don't get too rambunctious. Ol' Fido, he thinks**
26   **he's people.** *(Gets up to pour herself a cup of tea in pantomime.)*
27   **When I have the ladies over for bridge on Tuesday afternoons,**
28   **he greets 'em all at the door and then takes his place at the**
29   **end of the sofa while we all have our tea and cookies. Fido**
30   **takes his tea black and prefers the oatmeal cookies, don't you,**
31   **boy?** *(Returns to rocker.)* **His social graces aren't the best, but**
32   **Bessie and the rest of the girls don't seem to mind if he slurps**

1   a little from the saucer. Then, like I said, he snores all through
2   the bridge game, but we've gotten used to it.
3   Yes, sir, Fido thinks he's people. *(Sits back and rocks*
4   *contentedly.)* **Just rest easy, boy. Nothin' like a good fire and an**
5   **old friend.** *(Continues to rock as curtain closes.)*
6
7
8
9
10
11
12
13
14
15
16
17
18
19
20
21
22
23
24
25
26
27
28
29
30
31
32
33
34
35

5. The Actress

1   When I grow up, I want to be an actress. I know that
2 sounds dumb. Everybody wants to be an actress, but I can do
3 it. I *know* I can. My teacher says you have to believe in yourself
4 no matter what anybody says. You have to go for it! So I've
5 been practicing my lines. I got a part in the Christmas play.
6 I'm an angel. It's dumb, but I'd do *anything* to be on stage. Last
7 year I was a tree...a tree in the enchanted forest. So I guess I'm
8 coming up in the world. I don't know why they write plays like
9 that. Whoever heard of a talking tree? Well, I guess there was
10 a tree that talked in *The Wizard of Oz*. Now, there's a play I'd
11 like to do! I've seen it at least five times on TV. I could be
12 Dorothy. In fact, last summer my friend Brenda and I did a
13 show for the kids in the neighborhood. I was Dorothy and she
14 played all the other parts. I sang the songs 'cause she didn't
15 know the words.

16   I also had a part in *Oliver*. They did it at the little theater
17 downtown. I was one of the kids in the orphanage. I'm not too
18 good at dancing, but Mom says I can take lessons.

19   What I'd really like to play is Annie. You know, that other
20 little orphan with the curly red hair. *(Sings.)* "The sun'll come
21 out tomorrow..."

22   I like to go to the movies. Sometimes I pretend it's me up
23 there on the screen. Did you see *The Secret Garden* or *My Girl*?
24 I saw that one twice. It was so sad when that kid died. I think
25 it would be hard to pretend you were sad and cry while
26 everybody was looking at you. *(Stops to think.)* Actually, I guess
27 I've done it lots of times with my brother. Anytime things
28 don't go my way, I just turn on the tears. *(Demonstrates her*
29 *act.)* "Mom, Bobby won't let me watch TV. Stop it, Bobby. Ouch!
30 You're hurting me. *(Clutches her arm.)* Oh no! I think you
31 broke my arm."

32   *(Shrugs.)* When you're the youngest and the only girl, you

1   **have to learn some strategies, otherwise you never get to do**
2   **anything. Hey, no wonder I want to be in the movies! I've been**
3   **acting all my life. Watch this.** *(Starts to exit, coughing.)* **"Mom,**
4   **my throat's sore. Can I stay home from school today?"**
5   **Academy Award, huh?** *(Winks and exits.)*
6
7
8
9
10
11
12
13
14
15
16
17
18
19
20
21
22
23
24
25
26
27
28
29
30
31
32
33
34
35

6. Camp Cancanooga

1   *(At rise a GIRL is in her sleeping bag with a flashlight and*
2   *a candy bar.)* **Hey, Suz, are you asleep? Me either. Who could**
3   **sleep on all these rocks. Well, I did doze off for a while.**
4   *(Pauses and then answers.)* **Two o'clock...I wonder where the**
5   **others are. It's kinda lonely out here.** *(Pause)* **Yeah, I know**
6   **we're supposed to make it on our own for the next** *(Counts)* **six,**
7   **seven, eight hours. Don't you think we should make it to the**
8   **Point by ten o'clock tomorrow? I want to get there before the**
9   **others.**

10   **I'm starved. Got any of those beanie weenies left? Never**
11   **mind. I'll have a candy bar instead.** *(Opens wrapper and begins*
12   *to eat. Hears something to left.)* **What was that? Over there. I**
13   **heard something in the bushes.** *Bears!* **Some things are** *not*
14   **funny, Suz. Being a bear burrito wrapped up in this L. L. Bean**
15   **sleeping bag is not my idea of a good way to go. Besides, there**
16   **aren't any bears in these mountains.** *(Pause)* **Are there? I**
17   **didn't think so. Bears, blisters, bruises, bug bites. What were**
18   **my parents thinking?** *(Recites as if reading a sign.)* **"Camp**
19   **Cancanooga, wilderness training...we build character." Ooga,**
20   **Ooga Camp Cancanooga! Thanks a lot, Mom and Dad. I liked**
21   **my character just the way it was.** *(Pause)* **OK, you're right. It's**
22   **really not so bad.**

23   **So...what did you think of the obstacle course today?**
24   **Yeah, it was OK. You had to get pretty psyched to get on that**
25   **platform and fall off backward, especially when Jenny**
26   **Pheiffer was one of the ones catching you. She's a toothpick.**

27   *(Sarcastically)* **Oh, yeah, climbing the pole was definitely**
28   **the best. Twenty-five feet straight up! I'm not afraid of heights,**
29   **but that last step was a killer. There I was stuck at the**
30   **top...hugging that pole like a big koala bear.** *(Demonstrates.)*
31   **The big question was...how do I let go long enough to get my**
32   **balance and climb up on top of that thing? I know we had a**

1   harness. Still...I was petrified...really. I remember thinking:
2   OK, Cheryl, you can do this. Just get one foot on top. Easy does
3   it. Now the other foot. *(No response)* Now the *other* foot. It was
4   like that foot didn't belong to me. I was paralyzed! I mean, the
5   top of this pole is only about *(Measures)* this big around —
6   eight inches, maybe, and I'm supposed to get *both* feet on top
7   of there, balance and stand up. *(Laughs.)* Yeah, and then *leap
8   off!* *(Pause)* I don't know how, but I did it. I knew I could catch
9   the trapeze. I won second in state in the standing broad jump.
10 It was that last step on top of the pole. There was nothing to
11 hold on to. But I did it! Boy, if you can do that, you can do
12 anything. *(Pause)* Hey, I guess this stuff does build character —
13 whatever that is. Suz...Susan. I guess Susan is snoozin'.
14   *(Settles back in sleeping bag.)* Cheryl Sullivan...able to leap
15 tall telephone poles in a single bound. Ooga! Ooga! Today the
16 telephone pole...tomorrow the world. *(Yawns and stretches, lies
17 back.)* Good night, Suz.
18
19
20
21
22
23
24
25
26
27
28
29
30
31
32
33
34
35

7. Nothing Is Right

1   I give up! I tried out for the play. Hilary got the part. I
2   tried out for first chair clarinet, but Susan beat me. She also
3   managed to get straight As on her report card. I'm still making
4   Cs in algebra. I mean, all my life I've made As and Bs and then
5   I found out how stupid I am in math. Who can tell the
6   difference between x and y? And z stands for zero in my book.
7   Who cares? I never planned to enter Harvard on a math
8   scholarship.
9   But last week I also went out for cheerleader. I practiced
10   faithfully. I used to cheerlead in elementary school, so I
11   figured I had a pretty good chance. Every day I practiced for
12   hours. *(Demonstrates.)* I bent, stretched, and strained every
13   part of my body. And then...on the day of tryouts... *(Pause)*
14   Well, I guess I must have flopped when I should have flipped
15   or else my pompom pooped. I don't know what happened. I've
16   gone over it a hundred times in my mind.
17   What's wrong with me all of a sudden? I mean, I can
18   stand a little failure, but this is ridiculous! Suddenly, I can't do
19   *anything* right! Most of the time I've felt pretty good about
20   myself...till this year...and this year I'm a klutz.
21   Like yesterday in English class, I got up to do an oral
22   report and forgot the whole thing! Did I blow it? Does atomic
23   bomb mean anything to you? Well, I managed to scrape myself
24   off the floor and slink back to my seat.
25   I don't know what's going on here, but nothing –
26   *absolutely nothing* – I do is right!
27
28
29
30
31
32

8. Boarding School

1   *(GIRL enters left.)* **Boarding school...ha! This is ridiculous!**
2   **You board dogs and cats, not kids. First they pack you up, get**
3   **rid of all your most prized possessions, then they ship you off**
4   **to a place where nobody knows you and nobody wants to**
5   **know you. My roommate is some nerd in glasses named**
6   **Mercedes, not Mer-say-deez like the car, but Mer-su-deez. I can**
7   **see in about two seconds that someone like me may have a**
8   **problem in a place called** *(Curtsies)* **All Saints School for Girls.**
9   **Give me a break. No wonder they're all saints...there's** *nothing*
10   **to do around here.**

11   **My parents said it was for my own good...I almost flunked**
12   **the seventh grade. I've always been a good student, but this**
13   **year...I just didn't care.**

14   **Then there was the joke I played on M&M. What a joke...a**
15   *bad* **joke...and I guess that's really why I'm here. Some girls**
16   **don't know how to take a joke, especially Mary Margaret. I**
17   **wasn't too popular anyway, but after the incident with M&M,**
18   **I was a social outcast!** *(Innocently)* **All I did was hang her**
19   **bloomers on the flagpole. You know those little red tights they**
20   **wear under their cheerleader suits.** *(Snickers as she*
21   *remembers.)* **Oh, but it was wonderful!** *(Stands with hand over*
22   *heart.)* **Everyone stood up to sing the "Star Spangled Banner"**
23   **and there they were** *(Points)* **blowing in the breeze.**

24   **You see, I stole them in gym class right before the pep**
25   **rally. So when it came time for her to do her cute little**
26   *(Pantomimes)* **pompom routine...** *(Snickers again)* **well, little**
27   **Miss Mary Sunshine, queen of the rah rah girls, had to sit on**
28   **the sidelines till her mom could get there with another pair.**
29   *(Laughs.)* **And I made sure everybody knew M&M had lost her**
30   **bloomers. I loved it!**

31   **She thinks she's so cool. She is into everything**
32   **...cheerleader, student council. So this year when Jimmy B.**

1   started liking me, she couldn't stand it. You see, he's the
2   running back on the football team. Twice he made a couple of
3   good runs and a touchdown or two, and suddenly Jimmy B. is
4   a hero and Mary Margaret wants him. So she got one of her
5   friends to send him a note about how cute he was and how
6   much she liked him and how she wanted to invite him to her
7   birthday party. I couldn't believe it! She *knew* he had a crush
8   on me! Every day he walked me to class and sat by me at
9   lunch. *(Long pause)* But when M&M wants something...well...
10   *(Long pause, slower, with venom)* She got him all right. But
11   I...got...her! *(Pause)* And when everybody stood up for the
12   national anthem and Mary Margaret's bloomers went up the
13   flag pole, I felt *wonderful!*
14   *(Sheepishly)* It was just a joke. *(Shrugs.)* Oh, well...I hate
15   boarding school, but you know what? *(In a mean voice)* It was
16   *worth* it! And if I had the chance, I'd do it again in a minute!
17
18
19
20
21
22
23
24
25
26
27
28
29
30
31
32
33
34
35

9. Commando

1   *(GIRL enters right with doll and an umbrella.)* **Stop it! Get**
2   **away from me. I'm gonna tell Mama. Will so! Mama! John's**
3   **trying to make me jump off the garage. Ma-ma!** *(Slaps at him.)*
4   **No, you be quiet, John Jacob. Ma-a-ma! Make John stop**
5   **botherin' me.**

6   *(To John)* **I am not...am not a chicken.** *You* **are.** *(Makes a*
7   *clucking noise.)* **On guard!** *(Jabs at him with the end of the*
8   *umbrella.)* **Here...take that and that!** *(Screams and dodges him.)*
9   **A-r-r-g! No, you shut up!** *(Cackles again like a chicken.)* **You're**
10   **the chicken, John Jacob. So here...you take the umbrella and**
11   **you jump off the garage!** *(Taunting him)* **Yeah, big boy...what's**
12   **the matter?** *(Opens the umbrella.)* **You got a parachute. Go on,**
13   **chicken head! No!** *(Tries to keep him from taking her umbrella.)*
14   **Stop it. Leave me alone. Mama!**

15   *(Looks behind her where mother has entered.)* **Oh, there**
16   **you are, Mama. Make John leave me alone. This?** *(Holds up*
17   *umbrella.)* **No, Ma'am, I was not trying to hit him.** *(Pauses as*
18   *she listens to mother.)* **No, Ma'am, I didn't do anything to him.**
19   **He wanted to play Commando...Commando! That's when we**
20   **pretend to be paratroopers jumping off the garage and landin'**
21   **in enemy territory.** *(Listens again.)* **No, Ma'am.** *(Continues in*
22   *her most innocent voice.)* **I would** *never* **jump off anything. I**
23   **didn't even want to play this stupid game. It was John Jacob's**
24   **idea. Was too! Yes, Ma'am. Yes, Ma'am.**

25   *(Listens as mother reprimands John.)* **Yeah, J.J., you just go**
26   **on to your room and...** *(She stops short and looks at her mother.)*
27   **No, Ma'am, I didn't mean to be smart. Yes, Ma'am. I'll just play**
28   **over here with my dolls like I planned,** *(Moves to left)* **and we'll**
29   **have a nice little tea party.** *(She opens the umbrella and sets up*
30   *imaginary dishes innocently as she watches John and her*
31   *mother exit. She sticks her tongue out while mother isn't*
32   *looking.)*

1   *(Places doll under umbrella.)* **Now, you sit right here,**
2   **Betsy, and we'll pretend we're having a picnic at the beach.**
3   **Here, you can have some tea and I'll have some, too. It's such**
4   **a nice day.** *(Yawns.)* **We should have brought some sandwiches,**
5   **but have a cookie.** *(Yawns again and lies down on her stomach,*
6   *chin in hand.)* **Boy, is this boring! Who wants to play dolls? I**
7   **should have climbed up on the garage. Maybe we could push**
8   **the trampoline near the garage...John Jacob...John...** *(Frus-*
9   *trated)* **Oh, he's bein' punished for the next hour. Quiet time...I**
10 **hate quiet time! And now I don't have anything to do except sit**
11 **here.** *(She picks up the umbrella and looks right as someone*
12 *enters.)*
13 **Oh, hi, Suzie...Uh, playin' dolls. What're you doing? Here,**
14 **have some tea and a cookie.** *(Continues with a mischievous*
15 *smile.)* **Actually, I was just about to play Commando**
16 **...Commando. Oh, it's really not for girls, but John Jacob lets**
17 **me play.** *(Uses reverse psychology.)* **You probably wouldn't like**
18 **it. No, really. You're a little bit too...uh...short. Yeah, you see**
19 **this is a parachute and the garage over there is the**
20 **airplane...but, no, you stay here with the dolls.**
21 **Actually, this game is really too dangerous...for a girl**
22 **...any girl, except me. Well, I could let you help me move the**
23 **trampoline. That's the target. No, on second thought, you just**
24 **stay here and...well...are you sure you're not afraid? Of course**
25 **I've done it before...** *(Clears throat)* **lots of times. Oh, OK, if you**
26 **really want to. In fact, you can go first. Here, this will be your**
27 **parachute. Nothin' to it, Suzie. You jump and I'll be right here**
28 **to catch you.** *(Exits left with a sly grin.)*
29
30
31
32
33
34
35

10. Recital

1   This is my first recital and this is my new tutu. I wonder
2 why they call it a tutu. Maybe 'cause it's *too too* short. *(Pulls on*
3 *imaginary skirt.)* These are my new shoes...tap shoes...see.
4 *(Demonstrates.)* I like to tap. *(Continues tapping.)* A tap, a tap,
5 a tap, tap, tap. I like that sound. What I don't like is standing
6 in this line so long, trying to do what everybody else is doing.
7 It makes me tired. *(Squats.)* This is better. Now I can watch
8 while everybody else dances. I like recitals. *(Looking all*
9 *around)* Oh...there's my mom. *(Waves.)* Why is she looking at
10 me like that? She's doing this. *(Motions "get up" with her hands*
11 *as she imitates her mother. Tilts her head as if trying to*
12 *understand.)* What's she trying to say? *(Squints.)* What? *(Listens*
13 *and squints above footlight. Stands with hand over eyes looking*
14 *into the audience.)* I can't see anything with these lights in my
15 eyes. *(Cups her mouth.)* Can't hear you, Mom. *(Starts dancing*
16 *again, then tries to get in sync with others.)* Step, tap, shuffle.
17 Ball and chain, ball and chain. I love these recitals. *(Dances.)*
18 Hey, Mom, look at me! *(Dances in a frenzy.)* I'm dancing.
19 *(Continues, obviously improvising.)* This is great! *(Looks*
20 *around.)* Wait a minute...where's everybody going? I'm not
21 through yet! *(Curtain is closing.)* No, wait...wait! *(Opens curtain*
22 *and peeks through.)* That's all, folks!
23
24
25
26
27
28
29
30
31
32

11. Just Breathe

1   *(At rise a GIRL is sitting on the floor, legs crossed. There is a*
2   *stool On-stage.)* It's raining outside. I hate the rain. I hate the
3   way I feel on days like today – cold and gray – kind of hollow
4   on the inside – like there's nobody else in the world except me
5   and nothing to do. Mom says I need to learn to enjoy my own
6   company – learn to like my time alone. How boring! She told
7   me to try an experiment...sit in my room – no radio, no
8   magazines, and just try to be still for twenty minutes.

9   So, here I am. Now you've got to remember, Mom was a
10 flower child. You know, the sixties...Woodstock. Anyway, she's
11 cool, for a mom, I mean, but this quiet, calm inner thing is
12 weird. I can't get into it.

13   Like now. *(Assumes a yoga position.)* When I get very still
14 and concentrate on my breathing... *(Inhales and exhales*
15 *deeply)* I start to itch. At first it's just a little itch, here and here
16 and here, *(Starts scratching)* then suddenly my whole body
17 itches. But I keep concentrating *(Squeezes eyes more tightly*
18 *and makes a face)* and I breathe in a little deeper... *(Inhales*
19 *deeply, then exhales)* and out...in... *(Inhales)* out... *(Exhales)*
20 in...and besides seeing stars, *(Opens eyes)* I start to get this
21 movie going in my head. I mean, my whole life flicks by. There
22 I am...on the diving board, right before my swimsuit came off.
23 *(Pause)* And then I see Mom walking out to the patio with my
24 birthday cake, my tenth birthday, I think, then all of a sudden
25 I see my brother in the hospital when he got his tonsils out,
26 and in another scene I see Dad singing too loud in church.
27 He's tone deaf. All these pictures flash through my mind.
28 *(Pause)* And then I suddenly begin to worry that maybe I left
29 the oven on when I made toast, or maybe forgot to put the red
30 flag up on the mailbox. All this stupid stuff! And this is
31 supposed to be relaxing?! But I just hang in there *(Closes eyes*
32 *again)* and breathe. Push it out of your mind, Mom says. Let

1   everything go...and breathe. *(Continues inhaling, exhaling.)*
2   And just about the time I feel my shoulders relax and my head
3   start to bob a little, I start to feel this big lump *(Grasps throat)*
4   growing in my throat and suddenly I feel like I'm going to cry.
5   So I start to swallow and I can't. And the longer I sit still, the
6   more I want to cry. Wow, where did this come from? *(Opens
7   eyes.)* Suddenly, I really feel lonely and that makes me feel
8   afraid. What will happen when I go off to school? The boys will
9   graduate and they'll be leaving too. Then we'll all get married
10   and live our separate lives, and Mom and Dad will be getting
11   older and we won't be a family anymore — not like we are now.
12   Growing up scares me. There's so much I don't know, so many
13   decisions to make and...and...then... *(Closes eyes and inhales)* I
14   remember to breathe. *(Inhales.)* I keep saying to myself, keep
15   breathing, Jenny. Relax and be still. *(Exhales.)* Concentrate on
16   being here now... *(Inhales)* this minute. Relax... *(Inhales and
17   exhales)* and let go of all your worries. *(Long pause)* And pretty
18   soon, without knowing why, I begin to feel better... *(Inhales)*
19   and then I smell dinner cooking... *(Exhales.)* Mmmm. And
20   then I imagine my family around the table, talking and
21   laughing. *(Laughs.)* Dad is telling some story about my
22   grandfather, and my brother Stan is cramming too much food
23   in his mouth and there's Shawn, feeding the dog from the
24   table when Mom isn't looking. *(Inhales deeply, opens eyes.)*
25   And suddenly, I feel warm *(Pauses, wrapping arms around
26   herself)* and safe and happy inside. *(Laughs a little, surprised at
27   her transformation.)* Happy! *(Takes a deep breath.)* And it's still
28   raining outside! *(Laughs again and begins to exit.)* Well, what
29   do you know! It worked! Mom...Mom, it worked! *(Exits.)*
30
31
32
33
34
35

12. Tomboy

1   *(GIRL enters with baseball cap, glove, and a ball. There is a*
2   *stool On-stage.)* **I'm a tomboy. I'll admit it.** *(Hands on hip.)* **OK,**
3   **so what's wrong with being a tomboy? I can ride a bike better,**
4   **run faster, and shoot a B.B. gun better than any boy in my**
5   **neighborhood. It's not that I want to be a boy. It's just that boys**
6   **have more fun. Well, they do. I mean, dressing up and playing**
7   **with dolls are just not my thing.**
8   *(Pantomimes a girl playing with Barbie and Ken dolls.)* **Oh,**
9   **hi, Ken. I'm Barbie...Hello, Barbie. I'm your dream man, Ken.**
10   *(Rambles on in a monotonous tone.)* **Oh, Ken, let's dress up in**
11   **our beach clothes and ride in my Barbie mobile, and later on**
12   **we can dress up in our dance clothes and go on a date, and**
13   **after that we can dress up in our wedding clothes and get**
14   **married and live happily ever after in our Barbie dream**
15   **house.**
16   *(Sighs.)* **Give me a break! I'd rather be hikin' around**
17   **Goosepond Hill, playin' cops and robbers. Anything beats**
18   **playin' with dolls all day!**
19   *(Flops down on stool.)* **My dad says I need to act like a lady.**
20   **So how does a lady act?** *(Goes through the motions as she*
21   *speaks.)* **Am I supposed to sit up straight in a frilly white dress,**
22   **keep my face clean, my legs crossed, and my hands folded in**
23   **my lap? Please! Am I supposed to giggle, be shy, and look**
24   **pretty all day? How boring!** *(Gets up.)* **I'd rather be climbing**
25   **trees or hunting black birds.** *(Laughs as she remembers.)* **Last**
26   **year we made Earl eat one. Oh, we cooked it and everything!**
27   **He had to eat the bird to get initiated into the club. Me,**
28   **Bowser, Ray McKean, Sword Morgan, and Roger...he's Earl's**
29   **brother...we've got a clubhouse in the old tool shed over**
30   **behind Bowser's house. We've had this club for a long time,**
31   **since...** *(Pauses to remember)* **uh...sometime last year. Anyway,**
32   **we all go bike riding and sometimes we go swimming in**

1 Bowser's pool, and at night, just after dark, we like to play
2 flashlight tag and hide-and-seek.
3   Oh, I guess someday I'll gossip on the phone like my
4 sister Susan, and maybe someday I'll like boys and go on dates
5 like she does. *Yuck!* Well, maybe not. Imagine going to the
6 movies with Roger or Bowser. Well...I guess that would be OK.
7 But what about the part where we hold hands? *(Pauses, makes*
8 *a face.)* Kiss Roger?! Forget it! *(Pauses.)* I guess I'll just have to
9 be a tomboy for the rest of my life. *(Shrugs.)* Oh, well, I can live
10 with that.
11
12
13
14
15
16
17
18
19
20
21
22
23
24
25
26
27
28
29
30
31
32
33
34
35

13. Boy Crazy

1   Now let's get one thing straight...I am *not* boy crazy, and
2 boys are *not* the most important thing on the planet – not by
3 a long shot. *Clothes* are the most important thing! Just
4 kidding! Now that I've got your attention, let me say it again...I
5 am not boy crazy! Just because I stay on the telephone all the
6 time talking to this absolutely gorgeous guy in my English
7 class, and just because I've gone out with six different guys in
8 the last one, two, three weeks...does *not* mean I am boy crazy.
9 I just happen to like them a lot...a *whole* lot, and what's wrong
10 with that? I'm a teenager. Well, almost. My birthday is in
11 November...on Thanksgiving this year. And I'm thankful all
12 right. I'm thankful that Brian is finally beginning to like me.
13 He's the guy in my English class. Maybe he'll ask me to the
14 Christmas dance this year. Last year he was a short, skinny kid
15 with hair that stuck up like this. *(Pantomimes.)* And I don't
16 know what happened, but sometime during the summer
17 *(Pause)* Brian got taller and cuter. *(Pause)* A lot cuter! I didn't
18 even recognize him at first. He's been helping me with my
19 homework. *(Pause)* Not really, but that's a good excuse to call
20 him. Last night, we forgot to talk about English. I mean, how
21 much can you say about a pronoun anyway? But Brian? Now I
22 can talk about him forever. He wears the coolest clothes and
23 these little round sunglasses. Miss Randall makes him take
24 them off in class. She is definitely not cool...about anything.
25 *(Pause)* But Brian...well, he's weird, in a good sorta
26 way...different from any of the other guys. Since Brian came
27 along, I haven't even thought about anybody else. *(Pause)* Well,
28 except for Eric, but he's my sister's boyfriend. I've always had
29 a crush on Eric, and he's also got a friend named Charlie, who
30 plays in a band. I think Charlie's a sophomore...too old...*cute*,
31 but *(Pause)* OK, so I've thought about other guys, but...oh-h-h!
32 Wait a minute! *(Eyes follow someone walking across*

1   *Downstage.)* **Who's that? I've never seen him before. He looks**
2   **lost.** *(Straightens her clothes and fluffs her hair.)* **Maybe I should**
3   **go over there.** *(To the audience)* **Brian? Brian who? Just**
4   **kidding! But what's wrong with helping out the new kid?**
5   *(Shrugs innocently and starts Off Right.)* **Hey...are you lookin'**
6   **for somebody special?** *(Pause)* **The library? Hang on a minute**
7   **and I'll show you.** *(Exits with a wink.)*
8
9
10
11
12
13
14
15
16
17
18
19
20
21
22
23
24
25
26
27
28
29
30
31
32
33
34
35

14. Grandma's Things

1   *(GIRL holds up a locket.)* **This was my grandma's. If I look**
2 **really close I can see the letters engraved on it – LMD –Lou**
3 **Mull Drum 1922. That's when she and my grandpa got**
4 **married. She was a big German woman. My mother says I look**
5 **like Grandma when she was a girl. I miss her. She died around**
6 **Thanksgiving three years ago. I still think about her a lot. My**
7 **grandma celebrated everything with a big family dinner. I**
8 **guess she liked to cook, 'cause even on regular days when I'd**
9 **come to visit after school, she'd have hot brownies or fried**
10 **apple pies. She baked hundreds of pumpkin cookies, rhubarb**
11 **and gooseberry pies. I liked to go over and help her in the**
12 **kitchen. We'd can peaches, make watermelon pickles and**
13 **muskeydine jelly...things nobody heard of before. And**
14 **Grandma would tell me stories of the olden days when she**
15 **and her sisters would go to town on a buckboard pulled by a**
16 **team of horses. Her family were farmers. She said they were**
17 **poor, and her mama made all her clothes. But things were**
18 **different then. And Grandma didn't seem to mind. Anyway,**
19 **the best time she remembered was going to the county fair. It**
20 **took most of the day just to get there, and the ride was so**
21 **rough and dusty that she and her sisters wore dusters over**
22 **their petticoats and leggings and carried their dresses in a**
23 **sack to keep them clean. They took picnic lunches and**
24 **stopped along the river to take a rest and have their meal.**
25 **That was a long time ago.**
26   **She used to sit in this rocking chair that belongs to me**
27 **now. She'd sit and rock while I combed and braided her long**
28 **white hair, and she'd tell another story. I loved Grandma's**
29 **tales. She had pretty combs and beaded hairpins, and when**
30 **we finished, she'd take her hair that had caught in the silver**
31 **comb and wrap it around and around her fingers like this,**
32 **knot it like this and put it away. When I asked her why, she just**

1   said it was bad luck to throw part of yourself away.

2   In the winter when I'd spend the night, we'd sleep in her
3   big old feather bed with twenty dozen covers piled up high. It
4   was always cold in Grandma's house, so she'd take an iron —
5   the kind they used in the olden days, that looked like a big
6   chunk of iron with a handle — and she'd set it on the stove till
7   it got good and hot. Then she'd wrap it in a big towel and put
8   it under the covers at the foot of the bed. I felt safe when
9   Grandma tucked me in and slid in next to me. We'd say our
10 prayers and she'd tell me more stories...stories like the day
11 that Mavis dyed her hair and it broke off next to the roots. She
12 had to wear a wig — a red wig — for nearly a year. Stories about
13 Uncle Junior and the great snipe hunt...but that's a story big
14 enough for another time.

15   I'd hide caramels under my pillow and suck on them
16 while she'd tell the stories. She told me not to eat in bed, but
17 she didn't really care, I guess. 'Course I know she heard the
18 rattle of that cellophane on the caramels. But she never said a
19 word. My grandma loved me. That's why I liked to visit so
20 much. Being with Grandma was fun. We always did stuff
21 together. She never got mad at me about anything and she
22 always had time for a story, real stories about my family,
23 stories about Mother and ol' Bullet, the dog that saved her life
24 when an old mother pig cornered her in the barnyard.

25   I miss my grandma. I'm glad I'm like her, and someday
26 when I'm a grandma too, I'm gonna sit in this same chair, and
27 tell my granddaughter stories about the olden days when I
28 was a girl. I'll say, "Precious" — she always called me precious
29 — I'll say, "Precious, when I was a little girl like you, I used to
30 go over to my grandma's house every day, and she'd tell me
31 stories about the times Uncle Junior went snipe hunting over
32 near Swan Pond..." And I'll hold her and rock her...
33 *(Pantomimes holding and rocking small child)* and she'll feel
34 safe and happy...just like I felt when Grandma used to rock
35 me. *(Continues to rock imaginary child as the curtain closes.)*

15. I'm Shy

1   I'm shy. I don't wanna be but I am. It's not that I can't
2   think of anything to say. I have big conversations in my head,
3   and I'm a good writer. I just can't get it out. A brick has more
4   personality!

5   I think being shy just means being embarrassed all the
6   time, being afraid you'll say or do the wrong thing. Being shy
7   means being locked up inside and not knowing how to get out.
8   Sometimes I feel like I live in this really tiny bubble. I can look
9   out and other people can see in, but we can't touch each other.
10   *(Long pause)* I had a dream like that one time, only I woke up
11   and it wasn't a dream.

12   Before I moved here I had a friend named Jane. Actually,
13   she was a new girl at school...quiet like me. She had a horse,
14   and more than anything, I wanted a horse, and I wanted Jane
15   to like me. So...I told her I had a horse. Now, I know absolutely
16   nothing about horses.

17   "What kind is it?" she asked me. "Well, uh..." I
18   stammered around trying to think of something to say.

19   "Quarter horse?" She tried to help me out, but she knew
20   I was lying.

21   "Yeah, sure. Quarter horse." I felt so stupid. Why did I
22   have to tell her I had a horse?

23   She didn't say much after that, and I don't think she
24   liked me much either. I still feel stupid every time I think
25   about Jane. I wanted to write her a letter, but I didn't.

26   I wish I could be more like Charlie. I'm a good writer and
27   in all my stories there's a girl named Charlotte, but everybody
28   calls her Charlie. She's got lots of friends and they're always
29   off on an adventure.

30   I wrote a story about her sticking up for this guy named
31   Thomas. He was quiet and shy and all the other kids picked on
32   him 'cause he was a little fat. Actually, he was a lot fat. They

1   called him "lardo." He told the teacher, but nothing changed.

2   Then one day Thomas came into class late and just as he
3   was about to sit down, Billy Reynolds gave the signal, and
4   everybody bounced a little in their seats. Perfect timing. It
5   looked like Thomas had jarred the whole room just by sitting
6   down. Everybody broke up laughing when Billy said, "Easy,
7   Thomas. That was about an eight on the Richter Scale!"

8   Well, the teacher in the story scolded the whole class, but
9   the damage was done, and Thomas just sat there with his
10   head down until later in the period when there was another
11   big crash. This time it was Billy Reynold's turn to feel stupid.
12   He sharpened his pencil and went back to his seat, when
13   Charlie pulled the chair out and down he went with a thud.
14   Ha! After that, Thomas perked up a little.

15   *(Long pause)* I like Charlie. She always knows what to say
16   and do and she's not afraid of what others think. She's funny,
17   and she's smart.

18   I guess deep down I'm a lot like Charlie. I invented her, so
19   I guess she *is* a part of me. Now, I just have to find a way to let
20   her out and stop being so afraid. I'm tired of being shy. *(Pause)*
21   Today I'm going to change...and I'm gonna start by writing
22   that letter to Jane.

23
24
25
26
27
28
29
30
31
32
33
34
35

16. Separate Ways

1   Sarah, why are you ignoring me? Sarah? Sarah, will you
2   take those headphones out of your ears and listen to me?
3   Hello! I know you can hear me. *(Pantomimes jerking the*
4   *headphones off her friend and putting them behind her back.)*
5   There. Now you can hear me. No, I didn't break anything. It
6   just came unplugged, that's all. OK, here. *(Watches her go.)*
7   Hey, where are you going? Let's ride our bikes. You can ride
8   my new...What do you mean you don't like to ride bikes?
9   *(Pause)* OK, so let's go swimming. My dad just cleaned the pool
10   and... *(Sarah obviously doesn't respond.)*
11   Sarah, what's wrong with you? Are you mad at me?
12   *(Pause)* You *are* mad at me. What did I do? *(Pauses and begins*
13   *to beg.)* Come on, Sarah, tell me what's wrong. *(Pauses, then*
14   *begins to get angry.)* OK, so leave...go home and see if I care.
15   *(Turns her back, then realizes her friend is going. Goes after her.)*
16   Sarah, wait! How can I apologize if I don't know what's wrong?
17   Look, I'm sorry, OK? Whatever I did to make you so mad...
18   *(Pause)* What do you mean, I *should* be sorry? Oh...that.
19   *(Sheepishly)* Well, I didn't mean to...it just slipped out. You
20   know how you're talking sometimes...and your mouth just
21   flows over...and...Oh, Sarah, I didn't mean to tell Bobby
22   Farrington you liked him. He knew I was just teasing. *(Pause)*
23   How could you like him anyway, Sarah? He's a jerk. *(Pause)* He
24   is, too. He's always following you around, saying dumb things
25   to get you to talk to him. *(Pause)* No, I do *not* think he is cute.
26   All you think about is boys. We never do anything fun
27   anymore.
28   If it's not Bobby, it's somebody else. You've been in love
29   four times since last Friday. Oh, yeah? Well, last weekend it
30   was Jeff. Monday you were passing notes to Tim, and the next
31   day you practically chased Corey Jackson down the hall.
32   Thursday...what? *(Listens incredulously.)* *I've* been acting a

1　little immature lately! Well, excuse me, Miss Know-it-all, but
2　maybe you've been acting a little too grown up!
3　　　Oh, yeah, like riding bikes is *sooo* immature. *(Pause)* No,
4　I am *not* too old to be playing with dolls. You got a Barbie last
5　Christmas. And besides, I don't play with dolls, I just collect
6　them, that's all. Maybe you're a little too young to be wearing
7　makeup and writing love letters to every boy in class. *(Pause)*
8　You do too! I've been seeing that blue stuff on your eyes. So
9　what if Laura Mason wears it. It looks stupid! And I saw that
10　note. "Dear Tim, you are so cute. I have liked you since the
11　second grade. Blah, blah, blah." Gross! I don't get it. How come
12　all of a sudden you started acting weird? Last week at lunch
13　you and Laura practically ignored me. *(Pause)* Yes, you did.
14　You just sat there giggling and whispering and looking over
15　there where those guys were sitting. You did too! What do you
16　mean...just because boys don't like me? Who cares? You're the
17　one who's boy crazy! What? *(Pauses and suddenly makes a*
18　*change.)*
19　　　You're right, Sarah. What you do is none of my business.
20　I don't care what you do. And you can forget about swimming.
21　You might mess up your hair! *(Marches off.)*
22
23
24
25
26
27
28
29
30
31
32
33
34
35

17. Never Again

1   *(At rise GIRL is seated at a desk with a phone and a picture*

2   *frame, writing in her diary.)* **Dear diary, this hurts! They didn't**

3   **tell me it was gonna feel like this. Love, I mean. I guess it's not**

4   **loving...** *(Pause)* **It's knowing someone doesn't love you**

5   **back...even though he said he did.** *(Pauses and looks up.)* **I**

6   **think he meant it when he said it, but Cindy said he told her**

7   **he loved her, too. That was last spring, before they broke up,**

8   **and we started going out.** *(Picks up picture frame from the*

9   *desk. Gets up, paces a few steps.)* **I wonder how many people**

10   **you can really love...and how many times you *think* you're in**

11   **love before you really find someone special...** *(Slower)*

12   **someone you can love your whole life...** *(Pause)* **someone who**

13   **will love you back.**

14   **I think love is confusing. It makes you crazy all the time.**

15   *(Sits on desk.)* **You think about seeing someone, talking to him,**

16   **being with him. Sometimes that's all you can think about.**

17   **Nothing else seems important, and sometimes...well,**

18   **sometimes you neglect your friends...put them on hold or**

19   **cancel plans with them when he calls. It's not good, 'cause**

20   **friends matter, too. Like Melissa. She called me twice last**

21   **night just to make sure I was OK. She heard Mike and I broke**

22   **up. It was all over school. We didn't sit together at lunch, and**

23   **I avoided him in the hall. What was I supposed to say? "Hey,**

24   **Mike, it's OK. See this smile?** *(Plasters on a fake grin.)* **I never**

25   **really cared about you anyway." I feel so stupid. No, being**

26   **dumped is worse than being stupid. Your heart hurts and**

27   **there's nothing you can do...no way you can fix it...no aspirin**

28   **you can take...nothing you can do except pretend everything's**

29   **OK.** *(Long pause. Her mood becomes lighter.)*

30   **I don't know what happened. One day everything was**

31   **fine and the next day it was over...** *(Snaps fingers)* **just like that.**

32   **And I am sick and tired of feeling sorry for myself. From now**

1 on I'm through with boys. No more sitting around waiting for
2 the phone to ring. No more worrying about what to say or how
3 I look. No more boys ever again... *(Phone rings.)*
4   Oh, hi, David. *(Brightens.)* What's up? Yeah, we broke up.
5 *(Shrugs.)* No big deal. *(Pause)* Friday night? Well, actually
6 Melissa and I have already made plans. *(Pause)* Saturday?
7 Well, uh...hold on a minute, will you? *(Puts hand over the*
8 *phone.)* OK, this is it. *(Pause)* Do I go out and have a good time?
9 I like David. I've always liked David. *(Long pause)* Or do I stay
10 home and give up on boys forever? Do I want to go through all
11 this again? Oh, well, why waste a Saturday? Hey, David...sorry
12 about that. My mom was calling me. Saturday night? Sounds
13 great. Seven o'clock? How about 6:30? Maybe we could catch a
14 movie... *(She continues talking and laughing as the curtain*
15 *closes.)*
16
17
18
19
20
21
22
23
24
25
26
27
28
29
30
31
32
33
34
35

18. Playing Pretend

1   *(On-stage is a box with a tutu, a lady's hat, a shawl, a purse,*
2   *some jewelry, a safari hat, a white lab coat, and a motorcycle*
3   *helmet. GIRL shuffles in from left.)* **There's nothing to do**
4   **around here. I'm bored!** *(Looks at box.)* **I could play dress up**
5   **and pretend to be a ballerina.** *(Slips on tutu and leaps across*
6   *the stage, twirls, and falls on the floor.)* **No, I can't dance.** *(Trades*
7   *the dance costume for a hat.)* **Maybe I'll put on this hat and**
8   **pretend to be old Mrs. Ballinger in church.** *(Puts on the hat,*
9   *closes eyes and begins snoring loudly.)* **Or...I could be a lady, a**
10   **very *rich* lady** *(Puts on a shawl, a purse, and some jewelry)* **and**
11   **pretend I live in a very big house on the golf course, and every**
12   **year I go to Paris and buy lots of jewelry and fancy clothes, and**
13   **I drive a big car and...No, the truth is I'm a model, a high-**
14   **fashion model,** *(Removes shawl)* **and all day long I pose for**
15   **pictures in magazines and catalogs.** *(Struts across the stage,*
16   *turning and posing.)* **I have long shiny hair and I wear makeup**
17   **– lots of makeup – and everywhere I go, people ask me for my**
18   **autograph.** *(Pretends to be signing autographs.)* **Then I get a**
19   **starring role in a movie.** *(Puts on safari hat.)* **Yes, and it's a**
20   **movie about a girl who goes into the jungle to take pictures for**
21   ***National Geographic.*** *(Getting excited)* **Yes, yes! And all day**
22   **long I'll be taking pictures of lions and tigers and wild rhinos.**
23   **But then suddenly, the elephants stampede our Jeep. "Oh,**
24   **help, help, the elephants are stampeding!" So we hop into our**
25   **dugout canoes – yeah, yeah –** *(Pantomimes)* **and paddle down**
26   **the Amazon through the crocodiles and the man-eating**
27   **piranhas, but suddenly, the boat flips over and the crocodiles**
28   **and piranhas come closer and closer.** *(Long pause at the*
29   *thought of this scene.)* **Actually, I'm *not* a movie star at all. It is**
30   **my long-lost second cousin who looks a lot like me in the dim**
31   **jungle light.** *(Changes into a white lab coat.)* **I, on the other**
32   **hand, am a doctor – a very famous doctor – the best plastic**

1 surgeon north or south of the equator! I am the one they call
2 in to stitch up the wounds from the crocodile bites. After that
3 I pull one of the men off the rhino horn and save him from
4 the horrible jungle rot that invades his body. All over people
5 will say it's a miracle! *(Winding down)* It's a miracle... *(Digs*
6 *through the box to find a helmet; puts it on.)* Maybe I'll be a
7 motorcycle rider, or...an astronaut, *(Picks up steam again)*
8 blasting off to explore other universes, colonize other worlds,
9 off to...off to the kitchen. I'm starved. I wonder if we've got any
10 peanut butter.
11
12
13
14
15
16
17
18
19
20
21
22
23
24
25
26
27
28
29
30
31
32
33
34
35

19. Jackie, Libbo, and Me

1   Libbo's my buddy. Well, actually her name is Elizabeth,
2 but we just call her Libbo...Jackie and me. Jackie's my other
3 friend. She's a little meaner than Libbo. Maybe that's 'cause
4 she's a little shorter than Libbo. Jackie says people pick on
5 her, so she has to be ready to fight sometimes. Oh, she's ready,
6 all right. Might as well call her Eveready 'cause her battery
7 never runs down. That girl has more energy than me and
8 Libbo put together. Reminds me of a Chihuahua I once
9 knew...busy, busy, busy...always into something...tennis,
10 softball. She even took up karate one time. Won a first place
11 trophy that first year, and that was the end of that. If it comes
12 too easy, Jackie's not interested.
13   Libbo's the opposite. Everything's easy for her.
14 Well...maybe she just makes everything look easy. She never
15 takes anything too serious. Her attitude is, "If things don't
16 work out, oh, well...on to something else." Jackie stands her
17 ground. And me? Well, I just fume inside and feel sorry for
18 myself when things don't go my way. My daddy says I think too
19 much. Think too much? How can you think too much?
20   Oh, well, we're all good friends...me and Jackie and
21 Libbo. No matter what we do, we always have fun together. We
22 got a pact to always be there for each other, not to dwell on the
23 bad stuff, and always make each other laugh. When things are
24 really going bad or we're fighting among ourselves, we put out
25 our hands, one on top of the other, like a team, *(Demonstrates)*
26 and start saying "Pact, pac, pac, pac, pac, pact..." just to
27 remind us that as long as we got each other, nothing else
28 really matters. The way I figure it, laughing is the most
29 important thing. That and a good song. We're all good singers.
30 Jackie likes to lead, and I do a good back-up. "Rollin' on the
31 River" is our best number. We got a routine and everything.
32 Did it in the talent show last year. Would have won too, if it

1   hadn't been for Ben Blackmon and that stupid ventriloquist
2   act. I swear that dummy looked like Ben. You could see his
3   mouth move – Ben I mean – and none of his jokes were
4   funny...oh, well.
5   I usually sing harmony, but I got my solo specials, too.
6   "Summertime" is my best. *(Starts singing.)* My daddy loves
7   show tunes. That's how I learned the words to all those songs
8   nobody else knows. Blues songs. And when I start singing,
9   something good happens inside. I remember one time we
10   were going down the river. Libbo and Jackie were paddling
11   the canoe and I was hitched up behind on an inner tube. We
12   were having the best time laughing, dodging tree limbs and
13   stumps in the water, talking about all the things we planned
14   to do over summer vacation. And then we started singing
15   again, church songs this time. *(Starts singing "Swing Low*
16   *Sweet Chariot.")* It was beautiful. I mean we had the harmony
17   down and everything, and all of a sudden, Jackie burst out
18   crying.
19   Now, Jackie hates to cry, so we knew she had to be feeling
20   bad. We didn't say anything for a while, and pretty soon she
21   sniffed it all up and said that Boo had died. We felt really bad
22   'cause Boo was Jackie's favorite kitty. There was Sister and
23   Bubba, but Boo and Jackie grew up together. And that
24   morning when she called and called and Boo didn't come,
25   Jackie knew something was wrong. She went around to the
26   back yard and there was Boo laying under the live oak tree.
27   Jackie knew she was dying. You see, Boo had been sick a long
28   time, and Jackie just didn't want to let her go. This time,
29   though, she didn't run for her mama or call the vet. This time,
30   Jackie sat down under that big old tree and sang to her kitty,
31   till finally she quit breathing. All by herself, Jackie dug a little
32   grave, said a few last words, and buried old Boo under that
33   oak tree and put a Buddha there for a marker. Boo was a
34   Siamese, so the Buddha seemed right. *(Shrugs.)* Well, that's
35   what Jackie said.

1   And just about the time Jackie started feeling better,
2   Libbo started bawlin'. Nobody's heart is more tender than
3   Libbo's. She was hurting 'cause Jackie hurt, but then she
4   started thinkin' about her little dog, Annie. I said, "Annie's
5   just a puppy, not even a year old!" She sniffed and snorted,
6   "Yeah, but someday she'll die...someday we'll all die." *(Long*
7   *pause)* I knew she was thinking 'bout more than Annie. It was
8   kinda dark right then, even though the sun was shining and I
9   knew we were in serious trouble if somebody didn't say
10   something funny fast, but I couldn't think of anything. *(Long*
11   *pause)* And I guess sometimes good friends have just got to be
12   sad and sorry together.
13   About that time, Jackie stood up in front of the canoe, put
14   her hands out for the secret hold and started clucking to the
15   top of her voice, "Pact, pac, pac, pac, pac, pac..." Then Libbo
16   jumped up, but before she could get to Jackie, the canoe
17   flipped and tossed them both into the river. There we
18   were...laughing, choking, and doin' our pact...mostly
19   underwater. It was great! *(Pause)* You know, that pact thing
20   has helped a lot when nothing else seemed to work. *(Pause)* I
21   think everybody needs a pact with somebody else. Somebody
22   you can trust, somebody who can make you laugh, somebody
23   like Jackie...and Libbo...and me.
24
25
26
27
28
29
30
31
32
33
34
35

20. Moving

1	*(As the scene begins, GIRL is tearing up pictures and*
2	*tossing them in a trash can.)* **I'm throwing away all my pictures,**
3	**trashing my whole life. Oh, this one is me and Melissa at the**
4	**beach. What difference does it make? I don't have a life**
5	**anyway...not anymore. Dad came home today and said we're**
6	**moving. I don't want to move. Every time I get a few friends,**
7	**every time I start to like school...we move again. North**
8	**Carolina, Florida...this time it's somewhere in West Texas.**
9	**Who cares? Nothing matters anymore.** *(Begins to cry.)* **It's not**
10	**fair. This is my life, too. How can they do this to me? Mom says**
11	**next summer I can come back and visit. She doesn't**
12	**understand. Things change. By next summer, everything will**
13	**be different. Everybody will make new friends. They'll all be**
14	**going to high school. I won't fit in anymore.** *(Cries again.)*
15	**Oh, I hate this. I'm not going, and they can't make me. I'll**
16	**move in with Missy...stay here and finish the year. Her mom**
17	**wouldn't care. I'm over there all the time anyway. We're just**
18	**like sisters...better than sisters! Whoa, imagine no little sister**
19	**tagging along, messing up my room. I could stand life without**
20	**Julie for a while.** *(Becoming more hopeful)* **And then I could be**
21	**here for the spring dance and the track meets...and the eighth-**
22	**grade graduation. Maybe they could come back for that, and I**
23	**could go visit during spring break. It's not like we wouldn't**
24	**see each other, and maybe then...maybe...** *(Flops down*
25	*realizing the truth.)* **Maybe I better just forget about it and pack**
26	**my stuff, 'cause no matter what I say...about Julie, about my**
27	**parents...they're my family and I couldn't stay here without**
28	**them.** *(Starts packing.)*
29	**Here's another picture of Missy at the fifties dance. The**
30	**poodle skirt is her mom's. We had so much fun that night. She**
31	**spent the night, and we climbed out my window onto the roof**
32	**and watched the sun come up. We talked all night about**

1   everything. *(Long pause)* **Maybe she can come visit me this**
2   **summer. I know Missy. She'll** *never* **write, but maybe we can**
3   **call.** *(Continues packing. Emotion builds as she tries again to*
4   *convince herself.)* **We don't have to stop being friends just**
5   **because we don't live close. And when we go off to college, we**
6   **can still room together like we planned. Nothing has to change**
7   **if we don't want it to.** *(Long pause. She begins crying as curtain*
8   *closes.)* **Oh, it's not fair. I don't want to move.**
9
10
11
12
13
14
15
16
17
18
19
20
21
22
23
24
25
26
27
28
29
30
31
32
33
34
35

21. LaLou

1   LaLou is my sister. She turned four last week. It's hard to
2 believe it was four years ago when she came home from the
3 hospital. She was named after both my grandmothers –
4 Laura and Louise – but they call her LaLou for short. Cute,
5 huh? Not like Becky. Rebecca...it's my mother's name. I like it
6 OK, but no big deal.

7   I remember when they brought her home from the
8 hospital. Everybody brought presents to the house. My
9 grandma came to stay with us for a while. Usually she sleeps
10 with me, but she slept in the room with the baby. My mom
11 didn't feel so good, so Grandma took care of the baby till she
12 got better. At first, it was just like having a new toy. I got to hold
13 her and feed her and help give her a bath. Mostly she slept and
14 ate, but then she started crawling around, getting into
15 everything! Suddenly, it was my job to watch her.

16 *(Imitates her mother.)* No, no, LaLou. Becky, get your
17 sister. Wave bye-bye, LaLou. Becky, get the stroller. She's
18 crying. Becky, get your sister a baboo... *(Talks to audience.)*
19 Baboo...that's LaLou language for bottle. Ninie was her
20 pacifer. Buzz-buzz is her little push mower and Tatee is the
21 blanket she drags around everywhere. I'm serious.
22 Everywhere my sister goes, so does the blanket. LaLou, Tatee
23 and Chopper.

24   Chopper's our new puppy. Chopper loves to clamp onto
25 the ragged end of the blanket. We have lots of pictures of
26 LaLou dragging Chopper all over the house. In fact, we have
27 hundreds of pictures of LaLou doing everything you can
28 imagine – LaLou taking her first step, LaLou on the potty,
29 LaLou on her new tricycle with her Mickey Mouse ears, LaLou
30 with her hands in the birthday cake, LaLou in the back yard
31 trapping leprechauns. No, wait, this is true. They read a story
32 at play school about leprechauns, then yesterday, I went out to

45

1   the back yard and she had a shoe box propped up on a stick

2   with some strawberries inside...waiting for a leprechaun.

3   She's only four years old. It's pretty embarrassing to have a

4   genius for a sister. She can write her name and count to ten. I

5   also taught her how to sing the ABC song.

6   She loves Barney. You know, the big purple dinosaur on

7   TV. She's got these purple slippers with the Barney head on

8   top, and every time we turn on her Barney video, she puts on

9   her Barney slippers and dances in front of the TV. *(Imitates*

10   *LaLou as she sings and dances.)* "I wuv you. You wuv me. We're

11   a happy fam-i-wee..." She is so cute.

12   Yeah, I'm a little jealous sometimes. She gets all the

13   attention, but when she looks at me with those big brown eyes

14   and says, "Weed me a story, Sissy," I'm a sucker every time.

15   What would I do without her?

16   Hey, LaLou, let's watch Barney on TV! *(Exits singing the*

17   *Barney song.)*

18

19

20

21

22

23

24

25

26

27

28

29

30

31

32

33

34

35

22. Graduation

1   This is it. Five more minutes and I'll be out of here – free
2   – gone forever. Twelve years, a diploma in my hand and I'm
3   on my way to college – new friends and a new life. No more
4   high school. I'm giving up my pompoms, no more after-school
5   practice, no more summer camp and competition in the
6   blazing hot sun. No more skipping Mr. Davis's history class
7   and hanging out in the parking lot, no more food fights in the
8   cafeteria. No more Saturday nights circling McDonald's to see
9   who's out, no more cherry bombs in the girls' locker room.
10   That toilet looked like Old Faithful. I know it had to be Laura.
11   She looks innocent, but she hated Mrs. Jenkins for making her
12   run laps. No more fruit rolls in Mrs. Garrison's class. *(Laughs.)*
13   I'll never forget the look on her face when Jim Pearson
14   counted three and we all rolled apples, oranges and
15   grapefruits up to the front of her room. She was lecturing on
16   British literature...so boring, and then all of a sudden, there
17   she was standing in a pile of fruit. It was great.
18   We had some good times. The homecoming dance, the
19   prom. No more chaperons frisking us for who knows what. No
20   more "anonymous" notes from David McBride. He'll probably
21   find someone else in college. He was my first love. Look at him
22   over there. He's still the best-looking guy in the senior class.
23   *(Long pause)* And there goes Jenny, our valedictorian. If they
24   only knew she was the one who put toilet paper in Mrs.
25   Duncan's trees. *(Laughs.)* Well, I helped a little, but it was her
26   idea. No more senior trips to the beach and no more parties
27   after the games. No more jokes on the freshmen, no more
28   senior plays. *(Long pause)* No more fun...I don't want to
29   graduate. *(Frowns and puts hands over her face.)*
30
31
32

Part Two:

MONOLOGS FOR BOYS

Caught!

Benchwarmer

Spud

Charlie's a Nerd

Dracula at the Unemployment Office

Big Trouble

Wanna Be

I Love Summertime

The Frog Prince

Batman Has Amnesia

Mighty Mite

Welcome to Middleton

Superman Needs a Rest

Jilted

Just Say No

Cowboy

Mad Dog

The Hunt

23. Caught!

1   *(BOY enters. He has a grocer's apron hidden behind his*
2   *back, tucked into his belt.)* **I'm a thief, but I learned my lesson.**
3   **I mean it. Never again will I contemplate a life of crime. Not a**
4   **dollar loaned, not a pencil borrowed, not even too much**
5   **change given at the store. I'd give it back in a heartbeat. Better**
6   **than cringing with guilt and shame when the grocer says,**
7   *(Focuses to left and mimics grocer in a gruff voice)* **"Look kid,**
8   **either pay for that stuff or put it back."**

9   **"Who, me?** *(Struggles, in pantomime, to keep loot under*
10   *his shirt.)* **What stuff?" I say with wide-eyed innocence.** *(To left)*
11   **"Those peanut butter cups..."**

12   *(Aside)* **Obviously, he had missed the Butterfinger,**
13   **Fireballs and three pieces of gum.**

14   *(In grocer's voice)* **"And the Butterfinger, and the Fireballs**
15   *and* **the three pieces of gum you've got under your shirt."**

16   *(Sheepishly)* **Guess not. Hmmm. I was humiliated! What**
17   **had driven me to this desperation? It was my mother. I asked**
18   **for some money, but she said, "Not till you mow the lawn." I**
19   *mowed* **the lawn. Two weeks ago. I was starving! Just**
20   **one...well, maybe two peanut butter cups. I love peanut butter**
21   **cups. I don't know what happened. I got carried away. I just**
22   **kept putting stuff up under my sweatshirt. And then...I**
23   **dropped one.** *(Pauses, looks around for who might have seen*
24   *him; sighs.)*

25   **He saw me. Harley Simpson. Mr. Harley, himself. Owner**
26   **of Simpson's Feed and Grocery. Hometown store owned and**
27   **operated by your friendly neighborhood grocer. He lives right**
28   **down the street from us. Why couldn't it have been Winn**
29   **Dixie! We don't know anybody at Winn Dixie.**

30   **I was dead. "Sir, please don't tell my mother. I'll never do**
31   **it again. I promise. Please, Mr. Harley."**

32   **He eyeballed me for a long time. "See you in church**

1   Sunday." *(Long pause, shrugs.)* **That's all he said.**

2   **Dear God, help me! Sunday was five days away. What did**
3   **that mean? Pray for forgiveness? You're going to meet your**
4   **maker? Confess your sins before I call your mom?** *What*?

5   **Those were the longest five days of my life. I mowed the**
6   **yard...three or four times! Cleaned up my room. Took out the**
7   **garbage, hoping that maybe I could compensate. Maybe when**
8   **Mr. Harley called, Mom would remember some of the good**
9   **stuff, too. And every day I'd cringe when the phone rang,**
10   **cower when somebody came to the door and grit my teeth**
11   **when Mom called my name.**

12   **Finally, it was Sunday, and I woke up before daylight**
13   **with a knot in my stomach the size of a basketball. Judgment**
14   **day. Dear God, please...if you'll just let me get out of this one, I**
15   **promise I'll never steal anything again.** *(Pause)* **I waited, like**
16   **maybe I'd get an answer.**

17   **And I'll keep on doing stuff at home for my mom.** *(Pause)*
18   **And I'll go to church every Sunday, but not Sunday school. I**
19   **hate Sunday school.** *(Pause)* **All right, Sunday school, but not**
20   **church, not** *every* **Sunday.** *(Sighs.)* **Oh, please, I'll be good. I**
21   **promise.**

22   **We got dressed and drove to church that morning. I was**
23   **going to face my doom. Another week of waiting and**
24   **wondering would have killed me anyway. And there he sat,**
25   **Mr. Harley Simpson, right in the second row as you walk in**
26   **the door. He nodded and smiled. I looked at him and tried to**
27   **smile back, but I felt like dirt. Nothing was worth what I felt**
28   **right then. I just wanted to die and get it over with.**

29   **I remember the preacher talking about deeds well done**
30   **and how we need to love our neighbors as ourselves. He**
31   **seemed to be speaking right to me. Then I had a horrible**
32   **thought.** *(Gulp)* **Had Mr. Harley told the preacher?!** *Panic*. **Who**
33   **else might know? It was just a matter of time. My life was over.**

34   **At the end of the service, we walked outside, shook**
35   **hands with the preacher and I was just about to make a run**

1   for the car, when Mr. Harley appeared out of nowhere.

2   He waved and called out good morning to my parents.
3   Then he stood around and talked about a lot of stuff that
4   didn't mean too much until he put his hand on my shoulder.
5   *(Focuses to left.)* "Well, did Scott tell you?"
6   *(Focuses to right.)* "No, Mr. Harley. What were you
7   supposed to tell us, Scott?" My mom looked at me kinda funny.
8   *(Focuses to left.)* "Oh, I would have thought you'd have told
9   your parents, Scott."
10   That was the longest minute in my life. "Well, Mom..." I
11   cleared my throat. "Dad...I, uh..." I stumbled and stammered
12   trying to think of a way to tell them what I had been hiding
13   inside...what was gnawing in my guts. And just when I was
14   about to blow like a volcano, "I'm a thief. I stole some stuff at
15   Mr. Harley's store. I'm a dirty, rotten, no good, lying..." Mr.
16   Harley said, "I've asked Scott to come work for me. I let him
17   have some credit the other day so he could get a few things
18   and then we decided he could come work for me this summer,
19   and some days after school. If it's all right with you."
20   *(Lets out air like a deflated balloon.)* Whoa! Yes! I thought I
21   was gonna fall on my face right there. But I just looked kinda
22   stupid.
23   "Yeah, uh, Mom...Dad, is it OK?"
24   'Course they thought it was wonderful and I was busy
25   being thankful my life had been spared.
26   *(Putting on apron)* I never really thought about working
27   in a grocery store, but it's not too bad, really. I get a discount,
28   too. Well, I will after I pay off my "debt," and I have to put
29   some in the collection plate. Some promises I'd better keep.
30   But I learned my lesson, believe me.
31   Excuse me, Ma'am...paper or plastic? Oh no, Ma'am. We
32   don't take tips, but thanks for the offer. *(Pantomimes bagging
33   groceries as curtain closes.)*
34
35

24. Benchwarmer

1   I'm waiting for my dad. I've gotta tell him I didn't make
2 first team. Actually, I thought I did pretty good. I guess pretty
3 good just isn't good enough. John Donovan is better than me,
4 so is my cousin Nick. That's what really gets me. He's my
5 cousin, a year younger than me, about a foot taller than me,
6 and better at almost everything. He's the kinda guy everybody
7 likes to hang out with. So why does he have to humiliate me?
8 I'm serious. Last week at school, he started telling everyone
9 that I liked this girl named Christy, that I wanted to go out
10 with her. 'Course, Christy didn't know I was alive till Nick
11 started spreading all this stuff. Some girl came over and said
12 that Christy liked me, too. So at lunch, right before the bell, I
13 went over to talk to her, but she walked off real fast, and about
14 two seconds later I figured out the whole thing was a set-up, a
15 joke. Boy, was I an idiot!

16   So, here I am…feeling stupid again. Every time I stick my
17 neck out, I get the axe. I don't really care about football, but
18 my dad does. He was all-state in high school and played on a
19 scholarship in college. I'm not good at sports like he is, but I
20 do OK in school. I think he's proud of that, and someday I'd
21 like to be a doctor. *(Long pause)* But right now, *(Another pause)*
22 I can deal with Nick and the kids at school. I can deal with
23 being a second-string jock, but how can I deal with my dad?
24 How can I tell him I can't be something I'm not?

25   I hate this. Tomorrow this whole thing will be over. I
26 mean, I'll still feel bad about it, and Dad will probably make
27 some dumb joke about going out for the basketball team. He
28 knows I'm a klutz when it comes to basketball. But tomorrow
29 the worst will be over. He'll bring out all his old high school
30 videos, give me a few pointers, take me over to the field, toss a
31 few passes, run me through some plays, give me a few "atta
32 boys," and we'll both end up feeling better. But right now…uh,

1 oh, there he is. *(Looks off to left and waves; takes a deep breath.)*
2 **Well, there's only one thing to do.** *(Starts walking off.)* **"Hey,**
3 **Dad, good news is, you don't need season passes on the fifty-**
4 **yard line. Bad news is...well...** *(Pause)* **how 'bout a burger and**
5 **I'll tell you about it?"** *(Exits.)*
6
7
8
9
10
11
12
13
14
15
16
17
18
19
20
21
22
23
24
25
26
27
28
29
30
31
32
33
34
35

25. Spud

1   Well, this is it. Today is the class party. That was Spud's

2 idea. As long as I've known him, he's always had big ideas, and

3 most of the time, I've regretted listening to any of them. You

4 see, me and Spud have been friends since that first day at Miss

5 Mertie's Kindercare when he pushed me into the wall and

6 tried to take my Star Wars laser sword. Now you know, I'm not

7 a pushy guy, but *nobody* touches my laser sword, even today. I

8 knocked him down and held him until Miss Mertie came over

9 and put us both in a corner, facing the wall. I guess that's

10 when we really got to know each other. We probably spent half

11 our time in that corner. Like it or not, we got pretty close.

12   I remember the time Spud talked me into crossing the

13 street to McDonald's for a Happy Meal during snack time.

14 Miss Mertie turned her back to give Kimmie a cookie and out

15 the door we went, through the hole in the fence, and across

16 the street. We were munching on our fries, when I saw Miss

17 Mertie marching across the street with blood in her eyes.

18   Another time, we found some matches and some old

19 newspapers and built a gigantic bonfire out by the swing set.

20 We wanted to roast some hot dogs, but...well, the only thing

21 that got roasted was... *(Pauses and rubs behind.)* Like I said,

22 most of the time I regretted listening to Spud.

23   Next year, Spud and I will be going to different schools.

24 So I guess this will be the last time we get together. I'll be

25 going to Lakeland Middle School and Spud...well...it looks like

26 Spud will be going to some military school up north. In a way,

27 I guess he is finally getting what he always wanted...a sword of

28 his own.

29

30

31

32

26. Charlie's a Nerd

1   *(BOY enters with a soccer ball.)* **Charlie's a nerd, but he's**
2   **also my friend. He'd never tell you, but his I.Q. is 153. I heard**
3   **the guidance counselor tell our teacher that Charlie scored**
4   **higher than anybody who ever took that test at our school. Me?**
5   **Well, nobody said...and I don't want to know. Who cares,**
6   **anyway? What good is being smart? All Charlie gets is more**
7   **work and a lot of lectures about not living up to his potential.**
8   **I'd rather be a regular kid and let things slide once in awhile.**
9   **Don't get me wrong. I can do it if I try. Well, I *think* I can.**
10   *(Doubting himself)* **But what if I can't? What if I try as hard as**
11   **I can, and I still can't make good grades.** *(Deep sigh)* **That**
12   **would be the worst! Then everybody would know I'm stupid.**
13   **And then again...what if I did make all A's?** *(Pause)* **The next**
14   **thing you know, everybody would expect me to do it from now**
15   **on. I'd have to be perfect!**
16   *(Sits on the ball.)* **That's what happened to Jimmy. He was**
17   **goin' along just bein' a regular kid. He scored high on that I.Q.**
18   **test and started goin' to that special program with Charlie,**
19   **and suddenly Jimmy doesn't have time to do anything...except**
20   **study. All his parents care about is gettin' good grades. They**
21   **started grounding him for C's and he can't watch TV or play**
22   **ball till he's done all his homework. Used to...he's got to do a**
23   **lot more.**
24   *(Gets up.)* **Nope, being a whiz kid is OK for them, but**
25   **me...well...I think I'll just keep doin' what I've been doin'...and**
26   **right now, I've got a soccer game.**
27
28
29
30
31
32

27. Dracula at the Unemployment Office

1   *(DRACULA enters right and speaks to a character seated*
2   *Center Stage.)* **Excuse me, is this the unemployment office?**
3   *(Pauses.)* **Yes, I can read. Why do you ask? The sign on the door?**
4   **Well, excuse me for asking, but I don't see so well in the**
5   **daylight. I'm used to sleeping most of the day.** *(Yawns,*
6   *stretches, and takes a seat.)* **No, I did *not* lose my job because I**
7   **sleep all day! I happen to work the night shift. Every**
8   **night...for...oh, I'd say...about the last seven hundred years,**
9   **with no vacation, no sick leave and no insurance. So, please**
10   **don't insult me about sleeping all day. I happen to be *very***
11   **good at what I do!**

12   **Bloodshot eyes? Yes, my eyes are always a little too red,**
13   **but I've been working too hard lately.** *(In a sinister tone)* **And**
14   **speaking of blood...I'm about a quart low. Could you spare me**
15   **a little?** *(Pause)* **You gave at the hospital last week? That was**
16   ***not* what I had in mind.**

17   **And why do you keep looking at me like that? "Rocky**
18   **Horror Picture Show"? No, I am not dressed for the theatre.**
19   **I've never even heard of that show. But I am pretty good at**
20   **horror movies. Allow me to introduce myself. I am Count**
21   **Dracula. Watch this.** *(Gets up and makes a sweeping motion*
22   *with his cape and speaks with an accent.)* **Velcome to my castle.**
23   **I've been vaiting for you. Von't you stay for dinner?**

24   **Excuse me?** *(Pause)* **Werewolf impression? Look at these**
25   **teeth...this cape. Don't you recognize me?**

26   **No! I am not a rock star! I am a vampire! The greatest**
27   **vampire in all of Transylvania...I am Count Dracula!** *(Pause)*
28   **And you are who?** *(Pause)* **Frankenstein? Very funny.**

29   *(To himself)* **This man is an idiot. No wonder he doesn't**
30   **have a real job.** *(Sarcastically)* **Never mind, Mr. Frankenstein. I**

1 think they're calling your number. Good-bye and good
2 riddance! *(Watches him exit left.)*
3   *(Yawns and stretches.)* **Oh, what's the use? With**
4 **unemployment the way it is, I better stick with what I know.**
5 **Once a vampire, always a vampire.** *(Starts Off Right.)* **Taxi!**
6 **Taxi!**
7
8
9
10
11
12
13
14
15
16
17
18
19
20
21
22
23
24
25
26
27
28
29
30
31
32
33
34
35

28. Big Trouble

1   *(At rise BOY enters and sit on chair.)* **I'm in trouble...big**
2   **trouble. You see...me and Junior wanted to go fishin'. That's**
3   **how it all started, and I knew better. My mom's real strict**
4   **when it comes to some things. She thinks Junior's a "bad**
5   **influence," whatever that means. I think he flunked the**
6   **seventh grade a couple of times. That doesn't make him bad.**
7   **He goes to Carver Middle...when he goes. There's nothing**
8   **wrong with Junior except he doesn't care about**
9   **anything...except fishin'! And he's good at it, too. He even beat**
10 **ol' Mr. Jody in the bass tournament last year. Made the fishin'**
11 **lures himself. Junior's smart about some things. So, when he**
12 **started asking me to go fishing, I just had to find a way. The**
13 **trick was to get my mom to agree. I figured I might as well ask**
14 **her straight out.** *(Rises and focuses to the left.)* **"Mom, Junior**
15 **Parker wants me to go down to the river and fish a while this**
16 **afternoon. We'll just be gone a little while..."** *(To the audience)*
17 **Well, I didn't even get the words out of my mouth before she**
18 **hit the roof.** *(Imitates his mother and focuses to right.)* **"Now**
19 **you listen to me, young man. We've had this conversation**
20 **before and you have no business hanging out with Junior**
21 **Parker and certainly not around that river, not after that**
22 **Jones boy got sucked down in the current."**
23   *(He protests.)* **"But Ma, I'm not getting *in* the water! We**
24 **just want to do some fishin' from the bridge."**
25   *(Imitates mother again.)* **"Tom Terry, that boy is too old for**
26 **you, and you are not going down to that river...no ifs, ands, or**
27 **buts about it!"**
28   *(Sighs deeply, sits, and continues in his own voice.)* **Well, I**
29 **could see I was getting nowhere with that approach. I knew**
30 **right then, that somehow, someway, I was gonna get to that**
31 **river and sneakin' out seemed to be the only way.**
32   **That night I went to bed early, right after supper. Said I**

1   had a stomachache and was so tired I couldn't keep my eyes
2   open. Just to make it look good, I nodded off a couple of times
3   and nearly put my face in the mashed potatoes. Mom took my
4   temperature – she *always* takes my temperature when I act a
5   little strange. Then she tucked me in for the night.

6   Well, I gave 'em some time to settle in. Mom usually goes
7   to bed early and Dad snoozes in front of the TV, so I figured I
8   could be out and back before the ten o'clock news. *(Rises to*
9   *pantomime.)* I eased up the window just enough to crawl
10   outside, dragged my rod out from under the bushes where I
11   hid it that afternoon, and I was off to meet Junior at Sutter's
12   Grocery. Already, I could see a ten-pound bass chomping on
13   my bait. Ha, ha, Junior Parker...eat your heart out, boy!

14   By the time I met Junior and made it to the bridge, that
15   fish was about this long *(Measures with his hands)* and
16   weighed nearly twenty-five pounds – a world record! My heart
17   was beating so hard my head hurt.

18   We hadn't been there long when Junior offered me a
19   chew of tobacco. Now I knew better, but I took a big plug
20   anyway. *(Chews and spits.)* We were busy telling stories about
21   deer hunting down on Mrs. Myrtle's property; laughing and
22   spitting, when all of a sudden, something big hit my line and
23   for a few minutes it was just like I dreamed it! *(Pantomimes*
24   *catching the fish.)* I'd pull back on my pole and that fish would
25   take off. I'd reel in the slack and then he'd take off again.
26   Junior was screaming and hollering something and when I
27   started to yell back... *(Gulp and cough)* that whole wad of
28   tobacco went straight down my throat. Oh, man, I knew I was
29   a goner, but I just kept reeling and Junior kept screaming at
30   me just how to play him. Pretty soon I got to sweating. Then I
31   got hot and clammy all over... *(Slower)* and the more I'd reel
32   the dizzier I got. I knew it was gonna happen, but before I
33   could think, *(Bends over)* I was doubled up over the rail. *(Gags*
34   *and pauses.)* My rod and reel and that gigantic fish were long
35   gone somewhere down the river...and Junior Parker was

1   cussin' up a blue streak.

2   About a half hour later, after my whole body had turned
3   inside out, I was flat on my back trying to keep the ground
4   from spinning 'round beneath me. I had the flu one time and
5   thought I would probably die before I got better, but *nothing*
6   compared to this.

7   Somewhere in the back of my mind, I knew by now Dad
8   had flipped off the TV and Mom had looked in again to see if I
9   was all right. I knew I was dead anyway, so I guess at that
10   minute it didn't really matter what happened next. All I
11   remember was a siren *(Makes siren sound)* and some
12   headlights shining in my face and the sound of my mom
13   shrieking somewhere in the darkness, "Tom Ter-r-y! Tom
14   Ter-r-y!" I don't know what she thought — probably that I had
15   drowned or something. She flung herself down on top of me —
16   (Ugh) — and I lost my cookies again...if you know what I mean.

17   Junior explained about the tobacco and then he must
18   have disappeared in a hurry, 'cause after that my mom went
19   berserk. And sick or no sick, I got myself in the car. I heard her
20   apologize to the policeman...and the rest is history. *I'm*
21   history! My *life* is history! And I guess I'll be sitting in this
22   room till sometime next year...if I'm lucky.

23
24
25
26
27
28
29
30
31
32
33
34
35

29. Wanna Be

1   I don't fit in. I've never fit in anywhere. At school there
2   are the Surfers, the Jocks, the Preps, the Hippies...and me, a
3   Wanna Be, a group of one, a nobody. I'm smart, but who wants
4   to be smart? That's not cool. *(Sits down with a book.)* I like to
5   read and write stories. That's not cool, either. Besides, I want
6   friends. I want to belong somewhere. You have to be alone to
7   read and write, and I'm sick of being alone all the time. I
8   wanna be the one they choose first when we choose up teams.
9   I wanna look cool when I'm hanging out at school. My mom
10 thinks you have to wear shirts and pants that match – that's
11 not cool. I tried to explain about the grunge look, and the way
12 the guys on skateboards wear their pants down low and their
13 hair kinda long. My dad's an ex-Marine, so you can imagine
14 what he thinks about long hair!
15   I wanna be one of the guys that plays basketball after
16 school in the gym. I'm not really good at basketball. I just
17 wanna hang out with those guys. I don't care about being on
18 the team, I just want to hang out in the gym, talk to the
19 coaches, like they do...maybe be a manager and ride the bus to
20 the games.
21   I wanna be part of that group that hangs out in the
22 courtyard over by the trees at lunch. Those guys don't look so
23 cool, but Leslie is always out there, and Tanya, too. I'd just like
24 one chance to talk to Leslie Parker. She writes good stories in
25 my English class. The first time I was up front reading a story
26 I had written, she started looking at me...like maybe I was, you
27 know...somebody important. Ever since then I volunteer to
28 read my stuff to class whenever I get a chance. I've got a whole
29 notebook of stories. I write some poetry too. One is about
30 Leslie.
31   I wanna be a writer when I get out of school, go to
32 Harvard, get a good job, have a Porche and travel all over the

1   world. Money. I wanna make lots of money!

2   I wanna *be* somebody when I grow up. Trouble is...I don't

3   know where to start. I don't know how to be anybody but me.

4   *(Pause)* And most of the time...I'm just a *Wanna Be*.

5

6

7

8

9

10

11

12

13

14

15

16

17

18

19

20

21

22

23

24

25

26

27

28

29

30

31

32

33

34

35

30. I Love Summertime

1   (*Enters whistling, tossing ball and catching it in mitt.*) **I**
2   **love the summertime! Nobody owns you in the summer.**
3   **Nobody makes you go to school and sit still all day. Nobody**
4   **yells at you about doin' your homework. The days are so long**
5   **and you don't always have to go to bed even when you're not**
6   **sleepy and get up when you're still tired. Summer makes a lot**
7   **more sense. It's slower. It's hotter too. But I don't mind**
8   **sweatin' when I'm having fun. I like to ride my bike and go**
9   **fishing. I don't even mind mowing the lawn, but I can't let my**
10   **mom know that. She'd have me out there every other day**
11   **tweasing out the undesirables. My mother's lost it when it**
12   **comes to growing a yard. I like to play baseball, too, and go**
13   **swimming, but I'm not on the team. They practice too much.**
14   **Every morning at eight my brother Greg goes down to the pool**
15   **to do his laps. His specialty is the butterfly. He won most of the**
16   **meets in his division. Somebody always asks me how come I**
17   **don't swim on the team like my brother. How come I don't do**
18   **as good in school like my brother. But the truth is, I don't want**
19   **to be like my brother. I just wanna be me. And besides, what's**
20   **the use of having summertime if you still have to get up every**
21   **morning and *go* somewhere, *do* something, just because**
22   **somebody else wants you to.**

23   **Some days I like to lie in bed, read comic books or just do**
24   **nothing. I've got a great room upstairs. It's like a loft with**
25   **skylights. It's great in a thunderstorm – but I like it in the**
26   **morning too. I can lie in my bed and watch the clouds**
27   **changing shapes. There are a couple of squirrels that like to**
28   **play in the big gum ball tree that hangs over that window.**
29   **Sometimes I like to look out and not do anything. And**
30   **sometimes I don't think anything either. I just let my mind**
31   **hang out there – kind of limp. It feels great not to have to**
32   **worry about anything.**

1   Not for long though. I get itchy to get outside. The days
2   are so long in the summer you don't feel like you gotta hurry
3   all the time. Not like after school when you have to cram
4   everything into a couple of hours. There's never enough time.
5   So...today... *(Slams ball in mitt)* I'll play a little ball, ride
6   my bike to the little store down the street, buy an ice cream
7   sandwich, probably some Fireballs for later. I might go fishin'
8   at the lake over by Paul's house. You can't swim in it, but Paul
9   has a pool, so we'll probably swim a while and then...well,
10   who knows, there will probably be plenty of time left to do a
11   lot of stuff or nothing at all. I love summertime. *(Walks off*
12   *whistling, tossing the ball up and catching it.)*
13
14
15
16
17
18
19
20
21
22
23
24
25
26
27
28
29
30
31
32
33
34
35

31. The Frog Prince

1   (BOY enters in a prince costume or tuxedo.) **Oh, hi. If I look**
2   **a little green around the gills, it's because I am. Call it**
3   **paranoia; call it an anxiety attack, but this transformation**
4   **from frog to prince...prince to frog is about to get me down. I**
5   **mean, one minute I'm walking along, minding my own**
6   **business, and the next minute – b-o-i-n-g – I leap off toward**
7   **the lily pads! Sometimes I get a little warning before it**
8   **happens. First, I start to get itchy right behind the ears. I start**
9   **craving flies and my skin gets tight. And do you know how**
10   **long this has been going on? Years, decades, centuries even!**
11   **Every time some princess comes along looking for a prince –**
12   ***whamo*! – I get to be a croaker with bug eyes and weird-**
13   **looking toes.**

14   **I remember once I was right in the middle of a dinner**
15   **party down at the castle when I got that itchy feeling again.**
16   **Somebody had just passed the roast pig when I felt this**
17   **uncontrollable urge to leap into the fruit salad – b-o-i-n-g –**
18   **over the blueberry pie – b-o-i-n-g – across the candied yams**
19   **and into the butter – *splat*! The ladies were horrified. The kids**
20   **were all screaming and jumping around everywhere and**
21   **there I sat, right in the middle of the cabbage casserole with**
22   **butter all over my boots and a *really* stupid look on my face. I**
23   **mean, what do you say at a time like that? Thanks for the**
24   **invite? Sorry for the table manners?**

25   **Oh, no! I'm getting itchy again.** (Starts scratching and
26   pulling on his arms and legs.) **This is not good. My skin's getting**
27   **tight. I better get out of here while I still can.** (Said like a
28   hiccup) **Ribbit! Ribbit! Uh, oh!** (Starts walking off, then hops.)
29   **So long, folks. Ribbit! Ribbit!**
30
31
32

32. Batman Has Amnesia

1   *(Scene opens with BOY in Batman costume getting up off*
2 *the floor, dazed and confused.)* **Oh, hello, boys and girls! I'm**
3 **your friendly...uh, well...your not-so-friendly super hero —**
4 **able to leap tall buildings in a single bound — no, uh, that's**
5 **Superman. Uh...let me see...I know!** *(Holds up fist in the air.)*
6 **I've got the power! No, that's not it either. Let's see**
7 **now...Superman, He Man. How about — I am the terror that**
8 **flaps in the night — Dark Wing Duck? He's got wings, but**
9 **somehow I don't think I'm a duck. Oh, my aching head.**

10   *Zowie pow!* **I musta landed on my head when I jumped**
11 **off that building. I can't seem to remember anything.** *(Pulls*
12 *his mask up.)* **This mask is a little bit tight...cuts off the**
13 **circulation. Ears sticking out of my head.** *(Does some karate*
14 *move.)* *Zap! Pow! Bam!* **I don't get it! What's with the sound**
15 **effects? Either this is a bad dream, or I need a long rest. Maybe**
16 **I'm some kind of weirdo who acts like a regular guy during**
17 **the day and then —** *zamo!* **— at night he turns into a flying**
18 **freak who...** *(Looks confused.)* **A flying freak who...** *(Hits himself*
19 *on the side of the head.)* **Nothing! I just can't remember what**
20 **I'm supposed to do. Wait a minute...***zap, zud, zip***...and why do**
21 **I keep making those dumb noises? I keep seeing this stupid-**
22 **looking kid who wore a mask and funny boots...Blue Jay?**
23 **No...Sparrow...Chickenhawk...no. What was that kid's name?**
24 **Robin! That's it, Robin!**

25   **Now where is that guy and why is he following me? I also**
26 **remember some dude who looked a lot like a penguin. What a**
27 **nose on that guy! And besides being ugly, he was just plain**
28 **mean! Seems like he lived in the sewer. No way! I must have**
29 **lost some of my brains back on the pavement.**

30   **There's that searchlight again, and a giant bat. That's it!**
31 **The grand opening for K-Mart and I'm the main attraction.**
32 **Oh, no! What a letdown. Here I thought I was a super hero and**

1   it turns out I'm some clown who stands on the corner and
2   waves while everybody drives by. That's right. Last week it was
3   Shoney's...next week it's the new car wash on Main Street.
4   What a life! No wonder I tried to forget it. *Zowee zam*!
5   Well...it's off to work. At least it's a job. *(As he exits)* Attention,
6   K-Mart shoppers. Batman will be arriving in *(Looks at his*
7   *watch)* five minutes. *(Makes Batman music.)* **Batman!**
8
9
10
11
12
13
14
15
16
17
18
19
20
21
22
23
24
25
26
27
28
29
30
31
32
33
34
35

33. Mighty Mite

1   *(BOY comes On-stage Left dressed in football uniform*
2   *holding a football. He has play list in pocket.)* **Well, this is it!**
3   **Today I get to show 'em my stuff. I've got to prove to coach that**
4   **I'm the best quarterback he's got. Bucky's been playing most**
5   **of the time in practice, but last week during practice Coach**
6   **put me in. I threw a pass from the ten-yard line and we scored!**
7   **Then another time I did a quarterback sneak right through**
8   **the middle. That big kid Tommy tried to run right over me,**
9   **but sometimes I'm pretty slippery when I get the ball. My dad**
10 **said** *(Demonstrates)* **you just gotta duck your head, hold the**
11 **ball in close to your chest, and keep moving till you make it to**
12 **the end zone.**

13   **Ever since I can remember, I've wanted to play football.**
14 **When I was four, I got a football for my birthday. My brother**
15 **and some of the other guys played every afternoon after**
16 **school and I'd watch. Then one Christmas my dad got me my**
17 **own pads and a jersey from the Chicago Bears...a real one. My**
18 **mom wanted me to play T-ball and be on the Little League**
19 **baseball team, but I wasn't too interested in that. Then she**
20 **tried to get me into soccer, but that wasn't much fun either.**
21 **She knew I wanted to play football, but she thought I might get**
22 **hurt. That's when Dad stepped in and said I could be on the**
23 **Mighty Mites team. And here I am. Coach says I've got a good**
24 **arm.** *(Gestures like he might pass the ball.)* **And I can run fast,**
25 **too. This is the first game of the season, and all I want is one**
26 **chance...one chance to show 'em my stuff.** *(Paces back and*
27 *forth.)* **Dad says you gotta psych yourself up.** *(Slaps the football.)*
28 **Concentrate! Think about the game...just the game and**
29 **nothing else. Go over the plays in your head. Concentrate.**
30 *(Holds his stomach.)* **But to tell you the truth, I feel terrible. My**
31 **stomach is killing me, like maybe I might be sick or somethin'.**
32 *(Starts to breathe deeply.)* **But I just gotta concentrate, keep my**

1   mind on the game. *(Takes a deep breath.)* **OK, this is it.** *(Stops*
2   *suddenly, pulls a piece of paper from his pocket and studies it for*
3   *a minute.)* **Maybe I should write the plays on my hand. No, I**
4   **know what I'm doing.** *(Looks Off Left.)* **Hey, Coach! Wait up. I**
5   **want to ask you about this play.** *(Exits.)*
6
7
8
9
10
11
12
13
14
15
16
17
18
19
20
21
22
23
24
25
26
27
28
29
30
31
32
33
34
35

34. Welcome to Middleton

1   Hey, man, middle school is cool. No Charlie Brown
2 bulletin boards. Look, man, we got lockers and everything. No
3 more cubbyholes. No more reading groups and those dumb
4 smiley faces on everything. Miss Johnson musta majored in
5 smiley faces in college. No more lining up to wash your hands,
6 lining up to go to lunch, lining up to catch the bus. I hate
7 following behind a teacher like a bunch of ducks.
8   In middle school we get to change classes. That way if you
9 get a teacher you don't like at least you don't have to stay with
10 him or her all day. I wonder where I go to get my schedule. My
11 mom wanted to bring me to school today for registration. I
12 said, "No way. This is middle school, Mom." I didn't want her
13 hanging around. I can handle this. Trouble is I don't know
14 where I'm supposed to go. There are a bunch of guys – eighth
15 graders, probably – looking over here, laughing. I'll just be
16 cool. *(Walks to left.)* Hey, you guys know where I can pick up
17 my schedule? Orientation? Where? *(Looks Off-stage Left.)* Oh,
18 yeah. I see the door with the poster. Thanks. *(Exits left.*
19 *Screams and girls' laughter are heard Off-stage. He enters*
20 *looking embarrassed.)* Aw, man, that was the girls' restroom.
21 What? Welcome to Middleton... *(Laughs nervously.)* Yeah,
22 well...I guess I've got a lot to learn!
23
24
25
26
27
28
29
30
31
32

35. Superman Needs a Rest

1   *(From Off-stage)* **Up in the air, it's a bird, it's a plane, it's...**

2   *(Bounces in dressed as Clark Kent, with shirt, tie, glasses, etc. He*

3   *has a cardigan sweater tied around his waist. He brushes himself*

4   *off and straightens his tie.)* **...Superman! That's me! Able to leap**

5   **tall buildings in a single bound. Bet you didn't recognize me**

6   **in these glasses – nobody else does. Amazing how a pair of**

7   **specks can camouflage this face.**

8   **I was going to wear my leotards but my friend needed**

9   **them for dance class. Sometimes they get a little tight anyway.**

10   **Imagine wearing a stretch suit everywhere you fly. One or two**

11   **pounds and you look like a roly-poly with wings.**

12   **I mean, there's no chance of blending in with the crowd,**

13   **especially with a big red S on your chest and a cape flapping**

14   **around your neck. Sometimes I'd like a little peace and quiet**

15   **– R & R, if you know what I mean. And just when I get my**

16   **boots off and kick back in my La-Z-Boy, somebody starts**

17   **screaming for help. I mean there's no relief when you've got X-**

18   **ray eyes and supersonic hearing. And if it's not one tragedy it's**

19   **another – earthquakes, dams breaking, evil plots to overthrow**

20   **the government. After awhile even Superman needs a rest.**

21   **Being a hero is no piece of cake, let me tell you! Listen, I'd**

22   **gladly trade places with Big Bird or Barney. Or how about Mr.**

23   **Rogers. Now there's a laid-back guy. Just me and my cardigan**

24   **sweater, a song or two for the kiddies, and I'm finished for the**

25   **day. No more changing clothes in a phone booth, no more**

26   **drafty night flights. Sounds good to me.** *(Turns around to slip*

27   *on sweater, then turns back to audience.)* **Hello, boys and girls!**

28   **Won't you be my neighbor?** *(Freezes with hand in a waving*

29   *position and a big fake smile.)*

30

31

32

36. Jilted

1   *(BOY enters; has pen and pad in pocket.)* **I give up. No**
2   **matter what I do, it isn't enough. I write her notes in class. I**
3   **even wrote a love poem. Me...write a love poem? I'm not a**
4   **serious kinda guy, even when I'm asleep! But this girl has**
5   **really got me. I mean, it's like the last two years I haven't been**
6   **able to think about anybody else. Melissa...she's got big blue**
7   **eyes that sparkle when she smiles. Perfect white teeth. She**
8   **doesn't talk much, to me anyway. But she's smart in class. She**
9   **knows all the answers...in everything. Not that she's smarter**
10   **than me, but that's one of the reasons I like her. She doesn't**
11   **act stupid and giggle all the time like some of the other girls**
12   **in school.**

13   **She's talented, too. Got the lead in the school play. I**
14   **didn't know she could act, but now that I think about it, she's**
15   **kinda been leading me along ever since she figured out I liked**
16   **her. It really isn't a secret. I sit near her at lunch every time I**
17   **get a chance and I casually run into her in the hall every time**
18   **I can make it happen that way. I sit by her in classes that aren't**
19   **arranged in alphabetical order. Turner never comes**
20   **anywhere near Benson...Melissa Benson...** *(Sighs deeply)* **but at**
21   **least I can sit behind her and stare without her noticing.**

22   **I tried to get Mrs. Jackson to put me in the seat beside her**
23   **on the bus going to Sea World, but she made the guys sit on**
24   **one side and the girls on the other...like we were gonna make**
25   **out or something.** *(Laughs.)* **Yeah, like we might get away with**
26   **anything while Mrs. Jackson is around. Not that I wouldn't**
27   **kiss Melissa if I got a chance...** *(Sighs)* **just one chance. Like I**
28   **said, I didn't get to ride with her on the field trip to Sea World,**
29   **but once we got there, she and a couple of other girls did hang**
30   **out with me and these other guys. We walked around to the**
31   **Wild Arctic ride and went to the dolphin tank and the shark**
32   **tunnel. Then we sat down in the front row at the Shamu show**

1   and got soaking wet when that ten-ton whale slapped his tale
2   and created a twenty-foot tidal wave. It was great! She was cold
3   for the rest of the day, so I let her wear my jacket.
4   Later, at one of those ring toss games, I won this giant
5   polar bear. She went crazy, so I let her carry it around for a
6   while, knowing all the time I was gonna give it to her if she'd
7   take it. Oh, she took it, all right, and for a while she was really
8   nice. I guess she felt guilty about the bear. But not too guilty.
9   When it came time to get back on the bus to go home, I saw her
10 kiss Michael good-bye. He was one of the guys we'd been
11 hanging out with all day. Yeah, my good friend Michael. Some
12 friend! Anyway, she kept the bear. I didn't really want it.
13 Maybe when she looks at it she'll think about me. Yeah, and
14 laugh.
15   I ought to give it up, but I'm not done yet. She still hasn't
16 read my poems. Maybe that'll do it. What have I got to lose.
17 *(Takes out pen and pad. Starts to recite and write.)* "Melissa, you
18 mean so much to me. If only you could see what's inside my
19 heart, maybe then you'd start to feel the same. It's not a
20 game." Oh, man, I've really got it bad. This is stupid. I'm
21 stupid. Where's my self-respect? *(Sees her in the distance.)* And
22 there she goes...with Michael. And here I am trying to write
23 poetry to a girl who could care less. Hmmm. Something
24 doesn't add up here. *(Starts to write again.)* "Melissa..." *(There
25 is a long pause and a sigh. He wads up the paper and throws it
26 down.)* Hey, man...get a life! *(Exits.)*
27
28
29
30
31
32
33
34
35

37. Just Say No

1   Just say no...ha! I can say no to drugs, but what about my
2 brother? I don't even know who he is anymore. He looks like
3 my brother on the outside...well, sorta. He let his hair grow
4 longer and sometimes you can't see his face. It's like he's
5 hiding from something. He doesn't want to look you in the
6 eye, but when he does...sometimes it's like he's not even there,
7 like he doesn't see you. That's when he's really strung out.
8 That's when they take him away for a while. He's gone to that
9 place a couple of times...rehab, they call it. Rehab, as in
10 rehabilitation, as in get well and go home. Yeah, right!

11   He comes home all right, and for a while it's like it used
12 to be when we were younger. We play basketball and he takes
13 me places. We have dinner at night and watch TV. It's like
14 we're all trying so hard just to be normal, like maybe if we
15 keep up the act long enough we won't have to act anymore.
16 But then he starts coming home late again. They call and say
17 he's not going to school. The music gets louder, he gets
18 meaner and there's that look in his eye again. The last time it
19 happened, Mom couldn't wake him up. They took him to the
20 hospital and pumped his stomach.

21   He takes speed to get high and then he takes something
22 else to get back down again. He smokes dope, too. I've smelled
23 it on him when he comes in at night. I don't know what else he
24 does. They don't tell me much. I just get the usual lecture
25 about not doing drugs — "look what it's done to your brother;
26 look what it's done to our family."

27   I can't figure out what's so good about it that he keeps
28 doing it all over again or what's so bad about everything that
29 he just keeps getting high to run away from everything — me,
30 my mom and dad, school. Why doesn't he stop? Why did he
31 start? And this time he may go to jail. I think he needs to go to
32 jail for all the trouble he's caused. That's all my parents can

1   think about. We don't talk about it, but everybody knows. It's
2   like he's so bad that I have to do everything right to make up
3   for it – do everything perfect. *(Long pause and a sigh)* **Before**
4   all this started happening, I used to want to be like my
5   brother. He was good at everything, now he's nothing, dirt...a
6   loser...and sometimes...sometimes I wish... *(Puts his head down*
7   *and sobs into his arm.)* **I wish he'd just stop.**
8
9
10
11
12
13
14
15
16
17
18
19
20
21
22
23
24
25
26
27
28
29
30
31
32
33
34
35

38. Cowboy

1   *(At rise young COWBOY is practicing with a rope lasso.)* **OK,**
2   **easy does it. Get the rhythm, keep your eyes on the**
3   **cow...and...*release*.** *(Misses his target.)* **Close, but no cigar.** *(Pulls*
4   *rope back.)*
5   **I'm practicing to be a cowboy. You can laugh, but**
6   **cowboys still exist. Not here, but we went to a dude ranch in**
7   **Wyoming last summer and that's when I made up my mind.**
8   **Just as soon as I get a chance, I'm going to this rodeo school in**
9   **Texas, and one of these days I'll be a world champion cowboy.**
10   **I wanna do it all – ride and rope, make the rodeo circuit and**
11   **then with my winnings, I want to buy a ranch out West and**
12   **raise cattle for a living. That's what Shorty said he was gonna**
13   **do. He is one of the hands on the ranch in Wyoming.** *(Laughs.)*
14   **Shorty's about six-feet five-inches tall...about seven feet if you**
15   **count his hat. He wears a black Stetson and is big enough to**
16   **tackle any of the Dallas Cowboys. I don't know why they call**
17   **him Shorty, and believe me, I didn't ask. If Shorty wants you to**
18   **know something, he'll tell you straight out. He wasn't mean,**
19   **really...just quiet, one of those guys that looks scarier than he is.**
20   **One night after we had been out riding all day, I asked**
21   **Shorty about being a cowboy. Told him I wanted to be like him**
22   **and work on the ranch. That's when he told me about being in**
23   **the rodeo. He hurt his leg riding bulls, and I noticed he had a**
24   **limp when he walked. He said he was busted up pretty bad,**
25   **but he was going back one of these days. He told great stories**
26   **about bucking broncos and calf roping events. Said he was a**
27   **champion barrel racer at one time. Said it gets in your blood**
28   **and that's all you can think about, all you ever want to do. And**
29   **he's right. Ever since last summer, I've been thinking about**
30   **being a cowboy. That sounds kinda weird here in the city. Kids**
31   **ride bicycles and motorcycles. You got a fenced-in yard and a**
32   **dog if you're lucky. There's not much space when everything's**

1   a neighborhood or a shopping mall. Until I went out West I
2   never thought about how big the sky is or what it's like to ride
3   a horse across an open range. But even in Wyoming they got
4   fences now. Shorty says things are changing every day. More
5   people, fewer cows, more towns. Not enough open space even
6   for the animals.

7   So I gotta get out there and get some land of my own
8   while I still can. I gotta learn to ride and rope and be in the
9   rodeo, 'cause being a doctor or an engineer would be working
10 in an office all day and living in a subdivision. I never thought
11 about it before. *(Starts to rope again.)* But now I know. I mean I
12 really know it inside. *(Throws.)* That kinda life is not for me.
13 My dad says you can't make a living being a cowboy, *(Throws*
14 *again)* but I'm betting I can. And I'm gonna keep on
15 practicing... *(Throws again)* until I get it right.
16
17
18
19
20
21
22
23
24
25
26
27
28
29
30
31
32
33
34
35

39. Mad Dog

1   Hey, kid, see that guy over there? They call him Mad Dog.
2   No, wait. Don't look now. *(Nervously talks to keep the kid busy.)*
3   Here, take a look at this Kennedy quarter. See the numbers?
4   *(Begins to relax as he watches Mad Dog walk the other way.)* I know
5   it's not a Kennedy quarter. You think I'm a moron or something?
6   Only collectors have Kennedy quarters. No way, man. You can't
7   even buy a Kennedy quarter. I was just trying to save you from
8   Mad Dog. I know you're new around here, but if you'd like to
9   keep your nose in the same place, you better learn something
10   right now about Mad Dog. He's nobody you wanna mess with. I
11   saw him take a kid down just for lookin' at him wrong.
12   *(Demonstrates.)* You can look over, around, up, down...*anywhere*
13   but straight at him. And then it's best to look right over his
14   shoulder. *(Pause)* What do you mean *which* shoulder? His right
15   shoulder, his left shoulder! Just don't look him in the eyes,
16   'cause Mad Dog's got one eye that stays crossed most of the
17   time. And the weird part is...you can't tell which eye's the good
18   one. The other one is kinda cockeyed, too. *(Demonstrates.)* No,
19   man, don't laugh. It'll cost you your teeth and maybe your
20   whole face. I don't know if that's what made him so mean or
21   what, but he's big and he's bad and he likes it that way.

22   He used to play football but this is his third year in the
23   eighth grade, so he can't play on the team anymore. That guy
24   *shaves*, man. And I don't mean peach fuzz. Maybe that's why
25   he's so mean — anybody who has to spend three extra years in
26   middle school is bound to be pretty mad about *everything*.
27   But this year, he's outta here...no matter. Law says if you got a
28   beard you gotta go. No, you moron, I just made that up.

29   Uh-oh, look out, kid. Here he comes. Just pretend you
30   don't see him and let me do the talking. So, uh, kid, you're new
31   around here. Where'd you come from? Des Moines? Like as in
32   Iowa?

1   Oh, hey, yeah, Mad Dog. How ya been, buddy. Uh, no.
2   *(Digs in his pockets.)* I don't have a dollar. Fact is I only got this
3   Kennedy quarter. *(Laughs nervously.)* Well, I was planning on
4   borrowing a quarter from the kid here for a coke, but...The
5   kid? No, you don't have any money, do you? Five dollars? Hey,
6   kid, you been holding out on me! What? Sure, Mad Dog.
7   Uh...listen, kid, why don't you just loan Mad Dog that five
8   dollar bill? Lunch money...uh...well, you don't really need
9   lunch! Look at that extra tube you got around the middle. You
10   could stand to miss a meal. So...uh, why don't you just...Hey,
11   Mad Dog, wait a minute. He was just fooling around. Weren't
12   you, kid? He didn't really mean you'd have to take it from him.
13   He meant...Whoa! *(Watches as a fight takes place.)* Wait a
14   minute...Holy moly...What in the... *(Eyes stop suddenly on the
15   floor as he goes right to examine the body. Bends down.)* What
16   have you done? He's out cold. Down for the count. And you...
17   *(Gets up and turns to left.)* You! Where did you learn to move
18   like that? *(Dumbfounded)* I mean, one minute that big mutt is
19   in your face, and the next minute you're all over him. I never
20   saw anything like it. What? Black belt? Bruce Lee is your hero?
21   Hmmm. *(Looks back at Mad Dog.)* Listen, kid, what'd ya say
22   your name was? Gerald. So, uh, Jerry...is it OK if I call you
23   Jerry? *(Starts walking Off-stage.)* You're from Iowa, huh? I got a
24   cousin in Iowa. Listen, Jerry, you gotta show me how you do
25   that. *(As curtain closes)* Where'd you learn that stuff anyway?
26   They teach karate in Des Moines? Show me one more time
27   how you did that...
28
29
30
31
32
33
34
35

40. The Hunt

1   *(At rise BOY is sitting in chair with pen and paper on lap.)*

2   I'm supposed to write a report on my favorite pastime...three

3   pages on something I like to do when I'm not in school. One

4   thing I *don't* like to do is write reports...about anything. I don't

5   know what to write. I've been sitting here for twenty minutes,

6   and I can't think of the first sentence. I could probably tell

7   about things like canoeing down Blackwater River, or

8   camping in the mountains. But everytime I get my pencil in

9   position, I just can't get it to come out. It sounds so stupid.

10   *(Pantomimes writing.)* "Camping in the mountains is fun. I

11   like to go with my dad and my brother when the weather

12   turns warm." *(Pause)* And then I go blank. OK, so I try it again.

13   *(Pantomimes again.)* "Canoeing is my favorite pastime. When I

14   get a chance, I go down to Tomahawk Landing or Blackwater

15   River. It's fun to paddle over the rapids and around the tree

16   limbs in the river." *(Stops.)* One, two, three sentences. How am

17   I supposed to make that into three pages? Be descriptive.

18   That's what Mrs. Johnson tells us. "The beautiful water

19   ripples over the rocks, and I can hear the birds chirping as we

20   float along in the warm sunshine." It's not me. I can't do it.

21   Oh, my whole Saturday is ruined. It's not fair. So I got a D

22   in English. So what if I didn't turn in my homework a couple

23   of times? Now I have to get these progress reports signed every

24   week, and I can't go anywhere till all my work is done. But it's

25   the weekend! I can do this tomorrow! This afternoon my dad

26   and Doc Hardy are going over to Mr. McAllister's place to deer

27   hunt, and I can't go if I don't finish this paper. *(Getting more*

28   *frustrated)* Arrrggg! I can't do it! *(Crumples the paper and*

29   *throws it on floor.)* One more hour. He'll be leaving in one more

30   hour. *(Goes left and yells Off-stage.)* Dad? Yeah, I'm almost

31   finished. I just wanted to make sure you hadn't left without

32   me. Arrrggg. A new gun and I can't even use it – a twenty-

1   gauge. I got it for my birthday. It belonged to my Grandpa
2   Davis.

3   I killed a deer last year when we went. Actually, I didn't
4   really kill him – not right away. That was the hard part. We
5   were out in the woods about sundown. Dad put me on the
6   hunting stand by the big oak tree on the edge of that big field
7   after you go past the cattle gap. The deer like to come out and
8   graze right before dark. I'd been sitting there for what seemed
9   like a long time. My stomach was growling, and I had already
10   eaten my Hershey bar. I was a little bored, so I picked up a
11   stick and started digging in the dirt just to pass the time. I just
12   happened to glance up and there he was – not a hundred
13   yards from my stand, with a rack of antlers this big.
14   *(Demonstrates with arms.)* **For a minute I couldn't even**
15   **breathe. He was so big** – all muscled up, but *sooo* beautiful. I
16   don't really know how to describe him, but just about that
17   time I had my gun in position and his head in my site. He
18   looked up at me with those big brown eyes and in a flash he
19   turned to run back into the woods. At the same time he
20   moved, I felt myself pull the trigger and the kick from that
21   gun knocked me back against the tree.

22   The buck dashed off into the trees. I was pretty sure I hit
23   him, though. I let out a yelp like we do when we take a shot,
24   and I headed out toward the place where the buck had stood
25   a few seconds before. I looked around and saw the blood. My
26   heart jumped up in my throat. I got him, and there was a trail
27   of blood leading into the woods. That's the worst, 'cause
28   sometimes they run off and you can't find 'em. So I yelped
29   again hoping my dad would follow and help me find the deer.
30   I followed the blood trail probably a mile or two and there was
31   a lot of blood, so it wasn't hard. All the time I was following
32   him I had these feelings in my guts. It was like I was excited by
33   shooting a deer – my first buck – but at the same time I was
34   remembering his eyes and thinking about him running
35   through the woods trying to get somewhere safe.

1   I spotted him over by a bunch of limbs in a grassy place.
2   He was on his side still breathing, but it was easy to see he was
3   dying. I felt sick to my stomach and sorry that he had to suffer.
4   So I took another shot and he was still. I didn't have much
5   time to think after that. My dad and Doc Hardy were suddenly
6   standing beside me, patting me on the back, surveying the
7   size of the buck and asking me what had happened. I didn't
8   think of the deer after that. I had killed a buck! I had a story
9   to tell and that night at the camp I told it again and the other
10   hunters all had their stories to tell as we ate pieces of fried
11   venison — and talked about tomorrow's hunt. Dad cut the
12   horns off and told me we'd get them mounted and hang them
13   on the wall in my room, but I wanted them to be hung at the
14   camp. They seemed right at the camp, wrong in my room.

15   I don't really care if I kill another deer. There was
16   something I didn't like, but in a way I've felt bigger since then,
17   more grown up, I guess. More like my dad. *(Off left)* What?
18   Yeah, Dad, I'm just working on it. *(Gets his paper and starts to*
19   *write.)* I finally figured out what I want to write. I'll let you
20   read it when I'm through.

21   *(Starts to write and talks out loud.)* "It was opening day of
22   deer season. All year my dad and I waited for this day when we
23   could get in the Jeep and head out to Mr. McAllister's place.
24   More than anything I like to go hunting with my dad...
25   *(Continues to write and talk until curtain closes.)* I got a new
26   gun for my birthday, a twenty-gauge that belonged to my
27   grandfather..."

28
29
30
31
32
33
34
35

Part Three:

MONOLOGS FOR BOYS OR GIRLS

41. Bob, the Duck

1   Today for my show and tell, I'd like to introduce my best
2 friend. *(Looks Off-stage Right.)* **Bob, get over here right**
3 **now...Bob!** *(To audience)* **Excuse me, please. My friend Bob is**
4 **feeling a little self-conscious today. Bob, I told you not to wear**
5 **those bell bottoms. No, I have nothing against bell bottoms.**
6 **It's just that your legs are a little long or your pants are too**
7 **short. Actually, he likes to pull 'em up under his armpits.**
8 **Sorry, Bob!** *(To audience)* **He's too touchy about his appearance**
9 **sometimes.** *(To Bob)* **That's right. Come on over and stand next**
10 **to me.** *(Watches his/her imaginary friend cross the stage.)* **Boys**
11 **and girls, I'd like you to meet Bob...Bob, the duck. As you can**
12 **see, he's no ordinary duck. I know he wears his hair kinda**
13 **long. That braid in the back is especially nice, and he always**
14 **wears his little round glasses. John Lennon is his hero. He**
15 **reads a lot, and he's smart, too. Don't blush, Bob, you know it's**
16 **true. As I said, sometimes he's too self-conscious. Actually, he**
17 **wanted to be a hippie, but like me, he was born too late. We**
18 **both write poetry, but Bob can play the guitar. He knows all**
19 **the songs from the sixties.**

20   *(To Bob)* **What? No, Bob, you can't sing a song now. Don't**
21 **pout. You look stupid when you curl your bill like that, and**
22 **stop sticking out your tongue.** *(To the audience)* **Sometimes**
23 **Bob can be a real brat. I have to remind my mother that Bob**
24 **has a temper. Every time she raises her voice and gets mad at**
25 **me, he starts quacking to the top of his lungs. She also gets**
26 **mad when I feed Bob my broccoli and those little green peas**
27 **that make me gag. But he loves those things, so why shouldn't**
28 **he have them?**

29   **At night when I'm scared, Bob sleeps under my bed, for**
30 **protection, of course. We all know monsters hide under the**
31 **bed at night. But not when Bob's around. Actually, he'd rather**
32 **sleep on the bed beside me, and most of the time I let him. But**

1   when I'm afraid, he takes his place, no questions asked. Bob's
2   a friend that way. If only he didn't snore... *(Looks at Bob.)*
3   Sorry, Bob, I didn't mean to embarrass you again.
4   I think he might need his tonsils removed. In fact, when
5   they take mine out next week, I'm gonna make sure that he
6   gets his removed, too. But don't worry, Bob. They say we can
7   have lots of ice cream. No, Bob, really it doesn't hurt much at
8   all. They just take a pair of scissors and snip, snip...and it's all
9   over. A couple of stitches and... *(Watches as Bob exits.)*
10   Bob...Bob? Get back here! That duck is nothing but a big
11   chicken. Bob! Excuse me, please, I have a duck to catch. *(Runs*
12   *off right.)* Bob! Hey, Bob...wait up, buddy!
13
14
15
16
17
18
19
20
21
22
23
24
25
26
27
28
29
30
31
32
33
34
35

42. Beginning Again

1   My parents are getting a divorce. They told my brother
2   and me after dinner one night last week. I've been sick ever
3   since. Everything that goes down, comes back up. I'm not
4   hungry anyway. Who cares about food when your life is falling
5   apart. "Falling apart is what has to happen before things can
6   fall back together again." Some dumb teacher said that in
7   class one day. She talked about endings being new beginnings.
8   But I don't want things to change. What's going to happen to
9   my family? My dad's not living with us anymore and Mom is
10   going back to work. Oh, I can take care of Jimmy, but who will
11   take care of me?

12   Dad says everything will be OK. He says that he and Mom
13   still love my brother and me. Problem is...they don't love each
14   other. I thought love was forever, sorta like your I.Q.

15   I used to hear them argue at night when they thought we
16   were asleep. Mom says all people fight, but she gets mad when
17   Jimmy and I do. Maybe that's the reason Dad is leaving. Maybe
18   if we promised to get along better...Maybe if we cleaned up the
19   kitchen and promised to keep our rooms clean...Oh, I wish we
20   hadn't yelled at each other so much.

21   I wish it could be like that time when we went on
22   vacation to Disney World. Dad took Jimmy and me on Space
23   Mountain and Mom got somebody to take some pictures of us
24   at Sleeping Beauty's Castle. We laughed a lot back then. *(Long*
25   *pause as he/she remembers.)* And then there was the time we
26   all went camping on the river, *(Starts laughing)* and the
27   raccoons raided the picnic table while we were canoeing.
28   *(Long pause)* We used to laugh about everything...I don't know
29   what happened. When did we stop laughing? When did we all
30   give up?

31

32

43. New Puppy

1   *(CHARACTER enters right, whistling, calling for Harold.)*
2 I have a new puppy...Harold. He's about this tall, *(Measures*
3 *from the floor)* and his legs are about this long. My dad wanted
4 to call him Manfred or Riley or some other dumb name.
5 Harold's a Scottie, registered and everything. We've always
6 had mutts before, but this time we went to a puppy farm,
7 picked out Harold and paid the man big bucks for something
8 called a pedigree. It just means he's registered...where or for
9 what, I don't really know. I told Mom that now she wasn't the
10 only one in the family with a degree. She always makes a big
11 deal about going to college. It was a joke, but she didn't think
12 it was funny, about her and Harold both having a degree.
13 Sometimes she's too serious about everything.
14   Anyway, Harold is official and I like him a lot. He's really
15 smart, too. *(Pantomimes holding leash.)* Like when we go for a
16 walk, and I don't hold the leash just right, Harold stops dead
17 still, cuts his eyes up like this, *(Imitates Harold)* and waits. It's
18 like he says, *(Hands on hips)* "Come on, kid. Can't you get this
19 right?" And if I try to lead him somewhere he didn't plan on
20 going, he stops again, legs stiff, *(Imitates with arm stiffened)*
21 toenails dug in. I guess the truth is *(Pause)* Harold takes *me* for
22 a walk about three times a day.
23   He can talk, too...No, really. I've heard him say donut as
24 clear as day. *(Imitates "row-rut." Embarrassed)* Well, maybe not
25 like that, but donuts are his favorite...that and granola. He
26 always begs at the breakfast table and Mom gets real mad, but
27 if I had to eat what Harold eats...well, I'd beg for food, too. I'm
28 serious. Once I tried that cardboard stuff...just a piece or two,
29 to see what it was like. *Yuck!*
30   Harold sleeps with me sometimes when he can get away
31 with it. He loves to put his head right on the pillow next to me.
32 He sleeps on his back, with his feet in the air. He'd rather have

1   his belly scratched than eat when he's hungry. He's also
2   got a spot right in front of his tail *(Indicates spot)* that really
3   gets to him.
4   Curly used to love that, too. She was our dog before we got
5   Harold. She used to back up to the car bumper and scratch
6   herself bald right on that same spot. She was a yard dog, not
7   like Harold. Curly was one of those dogs who bent double,
8   wagging her whole body every time you came close. She'd lie
9   down and beg to be petted. Harold acts like maybe you owe him.
10   Anyway, Curly had been in the family ever since I can
11   remember. Mom says she adopted us. She wandered into the
12   yard, we fed her, and she took up residence at the back step.
13   Every time you walked out the back door, that little brown and
14   tan pup was there to meet you. And she always looked like she
15   was grinning. You know, her lip would curl up a little over her
16   front teeth and she'd wag all over. Oh, she was friendly all right,
17   but she was a watch dog. She hated strangers and she was
18   especially protective of me. Mom says that when I was little
19   she'd follow me around, grab hold of my diapers and pull me
20   down so she could lick me. *(Giggles.)* One time, we all went
21   camping and I wandered off a little way. Mom said Curly
22   barked and corralled me back to camp. I was screaming mad,
23   but I think that was the day Curly earned her spot in the family.
24   After that, Mom started giving her a bath once in a while, and
25   on Christmas, we tied a big red bow around her neck and
26   invited her in for the celebration. She always had a present
27   under the tree. *(Long pause)* I miss that dog. We used to go bike
28   riding together, and when I'd go down to the pier fishing, she'd
29   go right along with me.
30   Then one day when I came home from school, she didn't
31   come to meet me in the driveway. *(Stands and focuses left.)*
32   "Where's Curly, Mom?" *(Spoken to audience)* I could tell by the
33   look on her face it was bad. She'd got tears in her eyes and I
34   started crying, "No, not Curly! Not Curly!" *(After a long pause,*
35   *he/she continues with tears in her voice.)* Curly was a little deaf

1   in one ear and I guess she didn't hear the car coming when she
2   went across the road. I never knew anything could hurt so
3   much. Mom cried, too. Then she said, "It's OK, honey. We'll get
4   another dog, a cute little puppy..." Well, I cut her off right there.
5   "Dog! I don't want another dog. I want Curly!" I didn't want to
6   love anything ever again. *(Begins to cry.)* What's the use?
7   *(Slower)* It dies and then it hurts too much. *(Long pause)* It hurts
8   too much to love something and then lose it.

9   That's when Mom got mad. She pushed me down in the
10 chair and held me there. *(Speaks as the mother.)* "Now, you
11 listen to me. You'd give up all the years of fun you had with that
12 dog? You'd give up everything Curly meant to you just because
13 you couldn't keep her forever? Nothing is forever. And it hurts
14 when it's gone. *(Softens.)* But you just have to remember the
15 good times, and all the love that little dog gave you. That makes
16 it worth the hurt you're feeling right now." *(Long pause)*

17   She held me a long time and it *hurt* a long time. *(Another
18 pause)* But after awhile, *(Pause)* it didn't hurt as much...
19 *(Brightens)* and then we got Harold. *(Shuffles her feet, sniffs, and
20 wipes her eyes.)* Well, I tried not to like him. Like I said, he's not
21 Curly. There'll never be another Curly, but then there's not a
22 dog like Harold either. One of a kind...he's special.

23   *(Long pause)* I guess when you love something, *(Pauses to
24 think)* that makes it special. *(Pause)* Or do you love it because it's
25 special? I guess it really doesn't matter. Where is that dog?
26 *(Begins to exit.)* Here, Harold. *(Whistles.)* Come on, boy! *(Exits.)*
27
28
29
30
31
32
33
34
35

44. Family Vacation

1   *(A bench is On-stage. CHARACTER enters left, books in*
2   *hand, sits on bench.)* **Oh, hi, Louise! Yeah, back to the grind.**
3   **Great outfit. New clothes are the best part of starting school**
4   **again.** *(Pause)* **The Bahamas?! Your parents took you on a**
5   **cruise to the Bahamas?!** *(Pause)* **No, I don't even want to tell**
6   **you what I did. Believe me, it was nothing to brag about. Got**
7   **up, ate, watched TV, ate, helped Mom around the house, ate,**
8   **read a book, ate. I probably gained ten pounds. Two months**
9   **and twelve days of nothing. Not that I love school, but**
10   **anything is better than summer vacation.**

11   *(Pause)* **Oh, yeah, we left town once or twice, but that was**
12   **worse than hanging around the house. When my dad gets in**
13   **the car, there's no stopping for anything! Like when we went**
14   **to see my grandma...fifteen hours we were on the road! Do you**
15   **know how long fifteen hours is when you have to go to the**
16   **bathroom? I mean, if you happen to sleep through a gas stop,**
17   **you're in** *big* **trouble. When my family gets in the car, it's like**
18   **we're in a race or something.** *(Pantomimes.)* **My dad grips the**
19   **wheel, grits his teeth and we're off...weaving in and out of**
20   **traffic.**

21   *(Mimics dad.)* **"All right, Helen, it's seven o'clock. Write**
22   **that down. We've come 479,000 miles since three o'clock on**
23   **twenty-two gallons of gas. Check the mileage and give me an**
24   **estimated time of arrival."**

25   **Jeez! My mom would have to be Einstein to figure all**
26   **that! But that's not how Dad sees it. Mom comes up with some**
27   **calculation. He gets this determined look. Little beads of**
28   **sweat pop out all over his face, and everybody knows better**
29   **than to ask any questions or move around too much. Those**
30   **last few miles get pretty tense.**

31   **I remember once we were stuck in traffic on this bridge.**
32   **Mom had just done her latest calculation, and I guess the**

1   figures weren't too good, 'cause Dad had a death grip
2   *(Pantomimes)* on the steering wheel and he was yelling at cars
3   on the highway. His face was red as a beet, and I could tell he
4   was just about to blow. Anyway, there we sat on this bridge
5   and my mom was saying, "Now, Robert, relax a little...we'll get
6   there." And I don't know why, but about that time my brother
7   decided to roll down the window and yell at the people in the
8   car next to us. He plastered on this big smile, waved real big
9   and said, "Hi, buddy! How's it goin'?" Well...that did it. My dad
10   blew up! He yelled at my brother, gave him a few swats and
11   ordered him to roll up the window. I wanted to die of
12   embarrassment. I guess we were pretty much zombies the
13   rest of the way. Oh, he was sorry and all that, especially after
14   my mom said something. We even stopped at Stuckey's. He
15   also promised we could go to Disney World next year. Yeah,
16   right! Do you know how far it is to Disney World? If we take a
17   plane, I might consider it, otherwise I'm going to summer
18   school! *(Pause)* There's the bell. See you at lunch!
19
20
21
22
23
24
25
26
27
28
29
30
31
32
33
34
35

45. Saturday

1   Saturday! My favorite day. There's no other day that makes
2   me feel like this. Sunday there's church and Mom cooks a big
3   meal. We all have to hang around for family day on Sunday. But
4   on Saturday, I can ride my bike out to Sam Tilley's pond, go
5   fishin', walk over to Pat's and play in the basement. Or some-
6   times Chris and I pack some baloney sandwiches, fill up our
7   canteens and take a hike out through Mr. Mashburn's field. We
8   go around to Goose Pond Hill and back. He's got an old barn out
9   there we like to climb around in and some old tractors and stuff.
10   One time we had lunch right in the back of one of his
11   brand new John Deere combines. We had such a good time that
12   day, singing songs, telling stories. And when I cut myself on the
13   barbwire fence, Chris pricked his/her finger, too, so we could
14   be blood brothers/sisters – Dusty and Rusty. That's what we
15   decided to call ourselves. We made up a song about the whole
16   day. *(Sings.)* "Hikin', hikin' ain't much fun, 'specially when you
17   have to run. Goin' through the mud, goin' through the briars,
18   ain't much fun when you hit those wires!" *(Laughs at the*
19   *memory.)* And these old cows came after us as we were comin'
20   across this pasture at the foot of the hill. By that time, the rain
21   had started to come down pretty good. Not that cows ever hurt
22   anybody. I guess they thought we'd come to feed them.
23   Anyway, we took off across that field, yellin' and
24   splashin' mud, and the next thing you know, we were in for a
25   shock – a real shock! We never expected that electric wire
26   strung up across that field. Now that I think about it though,
27   it made perfect sense – cows, pasture, fence. Well, we didn't
28   really hurt ourselves, but we did get a pretty good jolt and a lot
29   of laughs. I do believe it was the best Saturday ever. Yep, we
30   had a good time, all right. Maybe we'll go back there today!
31   *(Exits singing, "Hikin', hikin' ain't much fun, 'specially when*
32   *you have to run...")*

46. Night Magic

1   *(Walks in holding a flashlight.)* **I like to come out at night,**
2   **a cool night like this, when the sky is perfectly clear. I like to**
3   **sit down and get real still and just feel how big it all is. The sky**
4   **just seems to go on forever and ever – deep, dark and**
5   **mysterious, with millions and millions of stars and planets.**
6   **There's the Milky Way.**

7   **Sometimes I feel so small, like what difference can it**
8   **possibly make that I'm here and why am I sitting in my**
9   **backyard on planet Earth. I wonder if there's anybody out**
10   **there like me, wondering the same thing? Wonder how you**
11   **say "hello" in Morse code?** *(Flashes his/her flashlight off and*
12   *on.)* **Dot-dot-dash. Short-short-long. Our science teacher said**
13   **something about light waves traveling faster than sound and**
14   **going on forever and ever. But I think I need something bigger**
15   **than a flashlight to really communicate.**

16   **In the old days, before the world was all explored, you**
17   **just put a message in a bottle and somebody picked it up**
18   **another continent away. That was a universe away in those**
19   **days, but you can't do it that way anymore. The world is too big**
20   **and complicated.**

21   **I heard there is a lot of trash in space already from**
22   **people sending up satellites and balloons and other**
23   **experimental stuff. We're trying to communicate all right, but**
24   **we're trashing the great unknown before we even get to**
25   **explore it.**

26   **You know, on nights like this, I just wish I could stay a kid**
27   **forever, live out in the mountains where the sky is as big as**
28   **the ocean and people don't bother each other much.**
29   **Everything would be a lot quieter.** *(Slower, looking up)* **Every**
30   **night, I'd sit on the back porch** *(Takes a deep breath)* **and look**
31   **up at the stars...until my mother called me in. Gotta go now.**
32   **It's supper time.** *(Exits.)*

47. Running Away

1   *(As scene opens, CHARACTER is sitting on a stool, clutching*
2   *his/her pillow.)* **I'm grounded. I have to stay in my room till**
3   **Dad gets home. Then I'll get it for sure.** *(Rubs behind.)* **I've**
4   **been bad, but that's not the problem. I'm stupid. I'm so stupid**
5   **I can't believe how stupid I am.**

6   **You see, it all started when my mother wouldn't let me go**
7   **to Terry's house to spend the night. His/her mama said I**
8   **could, but Terry had chicken pox last week, and my mom said**
9   **I might get them too – if I went over there. That was dumb.**
10   **Everybody at school had the chicken pox except me. I'm never**
11   **sick. If the chicken pox was gonna get me, I woulda been sick**
12   **by now!**

13   **Well, I got mad and stomped into the living room to**
14   **watch TV. Then my mother came out of the kitchen and yelled**
15   **at me. She said I was picking on my brother. He told her I**
16   **wouldn't let him watch Mr. Rogers. He just wanted to get me**
17   **in trouble.** *(Pantomimes.)* **So...I bonged him on the head. He**
18   **screamed like I was killing him, and then I *really* got into**
19   **trouble. Mom yelled at me and made me go to my room till I**
20   **could behave myself. Humph! Behave myself! What does that**
21   **mean?** *(Pause)* **I wanted to go to Terry's...she wouldn't let me. I**
22   **wanted to watch TV. She wouldn't let me. Probably if I wanted**
23   **to go to the bathroom, she would have said no. She wouldn't**
24   **let me do anything!**

25   *(Gets up.)* **Well, I decided the best thing to do was run**
26   **away...then she'd be sorry! I sneaked some Cocoa Puffs out of**
27   **the kitchen, got a blanket and a pillow off my bed and**
28   *(Pantomimes tiptoeing)* **tiptoed out the back door. But then I**
29   **tiptoed back in again. I figured I better leave a note, otherwise**
30   **they'd probably be worried.**

31   *(Pantomimes writing a note.)* **Dear Mom, since you don't**
32   **love me anymore, I'm running away. Maybe I'll come back and**

1   visit later on, so please don't give my stuff away.

2   I wanted her to find it, but I needed time to run away,

3   *(Pause)* so I put it on the back of the toilet and two minutes

4   later I was out the door and off to...well...I didn't really know

5   where I was going. Maybe my grandma's house. But that was

6   a long way away and it was already getting dark. So I figured

7   I'd just spend the night in the garage. Nobody would find me

8   with all the boxes and stuff. We can't even park a car in there

9   anymore!

10   *(Sits.)* Anyway, I hunkered down in the corner next to the

11   washing machine behind Bubba's old bicycle. I sat on the milk

12   crate and ate my Cocoa Puffs, but I was still hungry. I could

13   smell dinner cookin' and just about then my stomach started

14   to growl. Suddenly, I was starving! I couldn't get comfortable

15   so I just sat there all scrunched up feeling sad and sorry for

16   myself. And then I remembered it was just about time for

17   cartoons. By that time I was really getting itchy, nothin' to eat,

18   nobody to talk to and no cartoons. I couldn't stand it! Maybe I

19   could leave tomorrow. Tomorrow would be soon enough. So I

20   decided to *(Tiptoe)* sneak in my window... *(Reaches for note)* get

21   the note and...*oops*! No note, no note anywhere! That could

22   only mean one thing. *(Long pause)* I was caught. And just

23   about that time, *(Big sheepish grin)* my mother walked into the

24   bathroom... *(Focuses to left)* "Hi, Mom, what's up?" I stood

25   there jiggling the handle. "Something's wrong with the toilet.

26   Hear that noise?" *(Another big grin)* I knew it was a stupid

27   thing to say but I had to say something!

28   Anyway, that's how I got here, and my dad will be home

29   any minute. *(Starts scratching. Pulls up shirt. Looks down.)*

30   Chicken pox! Oh, no! *(Sighs.)* What else can happen? *(Slumps*

31   *on stool.)*

32   Wait a minute! Chicken pox...sure! Nobody would kill a

33   poor little kid with chicken pox. Saved by a scab! *(Starts*

34   *scratching and whining.)* Mom...I don't feel so good. I think I

35   got chicken pox.

48. Gussie

1   I'm the only child. I haven't always been the only child,
2 but this year my sister went off to college. She said to look
3 after her stuff till she gets back, but I don't think she's coming
4 back. I mean, not for good. She visits on weekends sometimes,
5 but she really doesn't live here anymore. Suddenly, we got this
6 big house, and it seems so empty. Before my sister left, she
7 used to have friends here every day. They'd hang out in the
8 kitchen telling my mom all the latest gossip. It was like having
9 four or five sisters. The phone was always ringing. Once my
10 dad got real mad 'cause some guy called at midnight. We had
11 a big graduation party out by the pool, and a bunch of girls
12 spent the night. There were kids on the floor everywhere! It
13 was great! And then we took Cindy to college and everything
14 got quiet. My mom cried a lot. It's been a long time since I saw
15 her cry like that...a long time. It was when Gussie died. Some
16 things I don't remember so well 'cause I was little...five or six,
17 I guess, but some stuff you don't forget, even if you try. I guess
18 it's because Cindy's gone that we're thinking about Gussie
19 again. Gussie was my baby sister. I'm really the middle child,
20 like my dad. Well, I used to be. *(Long pause and a sigh)* Gussie
21 drowned in the swimming pool, and then there was just me
22 and Cindy...till Cindy went off to college.

23   I don't really remember how it happened. We were
24 outside playing by the pool. Cindy was on the phone, and I ran
25 upstairs to do something. I don't remember what. I just
26 remember my dad yelling and the ambulances. *(Long pause)* I
27 don't remember much after that till my mom told me Gussie
28 had gone away to be an angel in heaven. She was so little. I
29 wish God hadn't taken her. I want her here with me.
30 Everybody was sad for a long time. Mom cried every day. I
31 didn't want to sleep in my room after that. I don't know why I
32 was afraid. For a long time I slept with Cindy, till we got

1   Clancy, our cocker spaniel. He sleeps with me now, but
2   sometimes I still get scared.
3   I wish my mom would have another baby...a brother or
4   sister...I really don't care. We just need more people around
5   here. Cindy going away is like somebody dying all over again.
6   Well, maybe not as bad, but I miss her so much. One day when
7   I came down for breakfast, I saw my dad had tears in his eyes.
8   He was reading a letter from my sister. I got worried
9   something was wrong, but he was just missing her, too.
10   When I grow up, I'm gonna have a whole house full of
11   kids — five or six at least, and the last two will be twins so that
12   everybody will always have somebody to be with and nobody
13   will ever have to be alone. It's too sad growing up alone...too
14   sad.
15
16
17
18
19
20
21
22
23
24
25
26
27
28
29
30
31
32
33
34
35

49. No Nap Today

1   I love kindergarten. *(Gets up from desk.)* **Miss Pickford, I**
2 **drew you a picture. And here's another one I drew at home**
3 **last night.** *(Digs in her pocket for folded piece of paper.)* **This is**
4 **the Pilgrims and their dog Spot. Do you think Pilgrims had**
5 **dogs, Miss Pickford? Is that how dogs got to America? I bet**
6 **they came on the Mayflower.** *(Pause)* **Yes, Ma'am. I can sit**
7 **down.** *(Returns to seat.)* **I don't like sitting in this desk so much.**

8   **Will you tell us a story, Miss Pickford? When will it be**
9 **story time? Can I tell a story? I want to tell a story about my**
10 **dog named Parvo.** *(As he/she tells about Parvo, she fidgets in*
11 *and about her desk.)* **No, Ma'am, he didn't die, but he got real**
12 **sick. He's OK now. My daddy says he's hyper 'cause he's got**
13 **brain damage. Parvo can't sit still, Miss Pickford. Maybe I had**
14 **that disease Parvo had, Miss Pickford. I can't sit still, either.**
15 **Are you sure kids can't get *Parvo*? OK, if you say so.** *(Yawns.)*

16   **No, Ma'am, I'm not sleepy. My mat? I don't have a mat.**
17 *(Pause)* **Well, uh...my dog ate it. Parvo chews up everything. He**
18 **really does. He ate our hammock, too. Besides, I already had a**
19 **nap...this morning...right after breakfast. Yes, Ma'am, I'm sure.**
20 **It was right after I ate my Frosted Flakes.** *(To himself/herself)* **I**
21 **hate naps. This is the only part of kindergarten that's not fun.**
22 *(Yawns.)* **Yes, Ma'am, I'll be quiet.** *(Draws and yawns.)* **Miss**
23 **Pickford, when will it be snack time? After nap time?** *(Pauses.)*
24 **When is nap time over?** *(Pauses.)* **OK, OK, I'll be quiet.**

25   *(Begins to draw vigorously, then looks up slyly.)* **Ha! I**
26 **don't have to take a nap. They do and I don't.** *(Keeps drawing,*
27 *shifts in chair, yawns and stretches.)* **I hate naps.** *(Begins to*
28 *sink slowly into chair.)* **I'm too big to take a nap.** *(Yawns*
29 *and continues to draw.)* **I'll just draw a picture of Buckwheat,**
30 **my kitty.** *(Rubs eyes, head gets closer to the desk.)* **Buckwheat**
31 **under the tree...** *(Nods off.)* **with some flowers...Buckwheat...**
32 **and...Parvo...under the tree.** *(Falls asleep.)*

50. Spring Pageant

1   I hate these spring programs. Every year they make us
2   dress up in stupid costumes and sing stupid songs about trees
3   and flowers. And every year my parents come and take
4   pictures and tell me how great I did. Then I have to listen to
5   my brother tell me how stupid I looked. I *knew* I looked
6   stupid. Why do they lie to me like that? Why do they make me
7   do this? This year I was a butterfly. *(Goes into role.)*
8   Butterfly little flutterby *(Flaps wings.)*
9   Kissing tulip lips *(Throws kisses to the audience.)*
10   On your happy trips
11   To my garden by the sea *(Squats and flaps.)*
12   *(Gets up.)* You see what I mean? Last year I was a rabbit
13   hopping all over the stage, and in second grade I was a tree.
14   *(Holds arms out.)* The year before that I was a...frog. No, that
15   was in kindergarten. *(Thinks harder.)* Hey, cool! I can't
16   remember. Maybe in a few years I'll forget the whole thing,
17   but one thing is for sure. *(Pantomimes tearing off costume.)*
18   This is it for me. No more spring programs. Did you hear that,
19   Mom? No more! *(Starts Off Right.)* Now all I have to do is burn
20   those pictures!
21
22
23
24
25
26
27
28
29
30
31
32

51. Lucky

1   Lucky...that's my nickname. Actually, it's a joke. I'm
2   never lucky at anything. I carry a rabbit's foot. *(Pulls worn*
3   *rabbit's foot from pocket.)* Well, it is a rabbit's foot, even though
4   it looks a little like a...chicken bone. I've used it a lot...not
5   much hair left.

6   I remember once the Rams were playing the Redskins in
7   a playoff game...twenty-seven seconds left...fourth down on
8   the ten-yard line. We were all standing 'round the TV,
9   jumping up and down, screaming our heads off. "Touchdown!
10 Touchdown!" You have to know my family. We're fanatics
11 when it comes to football. Anyway, the clock was running and
12 the teams were at the line. "Touchdown! Touchdown!" I was
13 sweatin' more than the quarterback. The ball was snapped
14 and the quarterback dropped back to connect with the guy in
15 the end zone. Only he wasn't there and helmets were banging
16 everywhere. The whole thing was in slow motion.
17 "Touchdown! Touchdown!" Suddenly, I remembered the
18 rabbit's foot. If ever we needed some luck, it was now. I dug
19 around frantically in both pockets – a marble, a penny, a
20 ticket stub...the combination to my locker...a pen knife, the
21 house keys...these were *deep* pockets...a piece of bubble gum
22 and – *(He shouts these last words and jumps up and down with*
23 *excitement)* my lucky rabbit's foot! *Yes!*

24   I waved the rabbit's foot in the air and screamed to the
25 top of my lungs, just as the quarterback launched the ball.
26 "Touchdown! Touchdown!" But suddenly, *(Loud grunt)*
27 everything went black. I could hear the noise of the crowd but
28 above and beyond all of that was the roar of my father. He was
29 all over me! My face was buried in the carpet...rug burns on
30 my cheeks. *(In his father's crazed voice)* "Give me that rabbit's
31 foot!" Actually, he said a lot more than that, and he nearly
32 broke my arm!

1   *(Aside in a calm, thoughtful voice)* **Now, I wouldn't want to**
2   **stand on the line opposite any member of the Los Angeles**
3   **Rams, but let me tell you, being tackled by my old man was an**
4   **experience I never hope to repeat! Unnecessary roughing the**
5   **innocent kid with a rabbit's foot...that's how I would have**
6   **called the play and a penalty for foul language!**
7   **But back to the game. The ball was still in the air...high**
8   **and deep into the end zone and just about that time, from out**
9   **of nowhere, came some guy from the other team. He leaped**
10   **into the air like a high jumper, grabbed that leather bullet,**
11   **and in two seconds was running down the field to his own**
12   **goal post. No, not running – that guy was high stepping**
13   *(Demonstrates)* **like a show pony...football over his head for**
14   **everyone to see. Somehow he had escaped the masses and the**
15   **clock was on its last seconds...five...four...three...In the**
16   **meantime, my dad was doing his own high step...or maybe it**
17   **was more of a stomp. I mean,** *(Demonstrates with every word)*
18   **he was trying to pound that piece of rabbit fur into**
19   **smithereens. He yelled...** *(Still stomping)* **and he screamed,**
20   **"You and that blankety-blank-blank rabbit's foot!" He meant**
21   **to pulverize that paw and possibly** *(Gulps with a hint of fear)*
22   **grind me down with it. Me...his own flesh and blood...me...his**
23   **first-born kid! I was busy looking innocent and sorry as I**
24   **possibly could. Finally, my mom came to the rescue, handed**
25   **him a cold drink and led him back to the chair. In the**
26   **meantime, I snatched up my rabbit's foot and made a quick**
27   **dash for the back door.** *(Long pause)*
28   **Lucky? Well, like I said...** *(Happens to look down.)* **Hey,**
29   **look, a penny...head's up! Who knows? Maybe I am lucky after**
30   **all!** *(Exits.)*
31
32
33
34
35

52. Late Last Night

1   I'm tired. I stayed up too late last night. I watched an old
2   horror movie on TV and then I couldn't sleep. I hate to admit
3   it, but my mom was right. She said I'd be afraid. At first, she
4   said I couldn't watch it, but then I said, "Hey, Mom, I'm not
5   afraid of stupid stuff like that. I'm a big kid now."

6   I mean, it was a stupid show really. I don't know what
7   scared me. There was this spaceship with some big tall tin guy
8   who never said anything. He just zapped everybody with this
9   laser beam that came out of his head. I guess he was a robot.
10 Actually, the whole thing was pretty boring, till the end when
11 they tried to melt him down.

12   Have you ever noticed how for no good reason when the
13 lights are out in your room at night, all the stuff that *didn't*
14 scare you during the day comes rushing back to your brain to
15 haunt you in the dark? I got to thinking about spaceships and
16 aliens, not the robot kind but the kind with the bald heads
17 and the big black eyes, and suddenly the floors and doors
18 started to creak. No way I was gonna put my head out from
19 under the cover. In fact, I'd hold my breath every few seconds
20 to see if I could hear any other strange noises. I hate breathing
21 stale air, but the only defense against nighttime freak outs is
22 to stay covered up. Usually I go to sleep in Jenny's room if it
23 gets too bad, but I wasn't about to let anyone know how scared
24 I was. *(Big yawn)* So now I gotta pay, and I'm not sure it was
25 worth it. *(Yawns again.)* Stupid aliens. *(Looks around above*
26 *him/her, becoming more nervous.)* I take it back, guys. No such
27 thing as a stupid alien...or a mean alien, for that matter. Take
28 ET, for example. Now there's a nice alien... friendly. *(He/she*
29 *continues jabbering as the curtain closes.)* Someone you'd like
30 to know better. *(Laughs nervously.)* One of the guys...not even
31 touchy about his size...

32

53. Reverse Psychology

1   *(Enters and sits in last desk in a row.)* **Maybe if I sit here in**
2   **the back, she won't call on me today. I didn't do my**
3   **homework. I** *usually* **do my homework. Well, sometimes I do**
4   **my homework, but today...today she'll call on me. They always**
5   **call on you when you don't do your homework. I could**
6   **pretend to be helping someone else. Teachers like good deed**
7   **doers. Hey,** *(Taps someone in front)* **do you need some help?**
8   *(Pause)* **I don't know...just thought I'd ask.** *(Grins sheepishly.)* **I**
9   **could act like I'm copying something from the book. No.**
10   **Maybe if I just scrunch down and pretend I'm reading**
11   **something...No, wait...if I sit back here, she'll know I didn't do**
12   **my homework. Maybe I should sit in front...all the way down**
13   **in the front row.** *(Moves to front.)* **I'll look excited, like I just**
14   **can't wait to give her the answers. Teachers never call on kids**
15   **who know the answers. That's it. I'll sit right here and look**
16   **interested. Super interested. History is what I love most in the**
17   **world. I'll organize my papers...and...what? Chapter ten...**
18   **question one? Me? Well, uh,** *(Pantomimes shuffling papers)* **I**
19   **guess I didn't get that one.** *(Pause)* **Number two? Uh...question**
20   **number two.** *(Stalling)* **I'm sure I've got that one.** *(Pantomimes*
21   *shuffling papers.)* **Well, maybe not. A zero. I could do chapters**
22   **ten** *and* **eleven tonight.** *(Grins.)* **Double or nothing? Maybe not.**
23   **Oh, well.** *(Shrugs.)* **So much for reverse psychology.**
24
25
26
27
28
29
30
31
32

54. Chill Out

1   (CHARACTER enters, stands with hands on back of chair
2   he/she has carried On-stage.) Let's try an experiment. All right,
3   get comfortable, close your eyes, take a deep breath, and
4   pretend. Pretend you're a cloud way up in the sky...floating,
5   drifting. Now pretend you're a tree and your roots go way, way
6   down through the rocks and the sand and the different levels
7   of earth, all the way down to the hot, hot core in the center.
8   You're connected and calm down there.

9   Open your eyes. It's not really hot, and you're not really a
10 tree or a cloud. You're really a kid like me who is trying to
11 learn how to chill out. Anybody in here need to chill out? Oh,
12 there's a hand...and one over there.

13   Hmmm. How many in this room have headaches like
14 right here above your eyebrows or back here in your neck?
15 You know, the kind that pounds and pounds. Do you wake up
16 in the middle of the night worrying about all the stuff you
17 should have done the day before? Do you get mad really easy,
18 yell and fight a lot? I saw a few hands back there. Here's the
19 final test. Look at your fingernails. Do you have any? OK, are
20 they chewed down to nubs like mine? Ha! I see a lot of guilty-
21 looking faces.

22   I'm an expert on this stuff and Dr. Jameson says it's
23 'cause I have problems and I don't know how to deal with my
24 stress. Judging from all of you, I'd say this stress thing is an
25 epidemic! So what are we gonna do about it? Go to bed, sleep
26 all the time and try to forget about it? (Looks at someone in the
27 audience.) I see you tried that, huh? Me too, but you gotta wake
28 up sometime. Maybe you read a lot, watch TV, fill up the
29 empty spaces with food. (Puffs out his/her cheeks and stretches
30 his/her arms out in front to show how fat he/she can get.) I don't
31 think that works very well.

32   I know nobody here takes drugs, but maybe you know

1   someone who does. Yes, I see you do. Drugs and alcohol don't
2   solve any problems, but they sure can cause you some. Ask
3   those kids who got caught down at the juvenile detention
4   center. Ask the ones who have a habit they can't quit. They've
5   got problems on top of problems. And it doesn't matter what
6   the guy next to you decides. You've got choices. So what are
7   you gonna do? How are you gonna solve your problems? Take
8   care of your stress?

9   I've got a plan. First, sit down. *(Sits.)* You've got to learn
10   how to stop once in awhile. Just stop, especially when your
11   head is racing and you feel like you're gonna explode. *Stop.*
12   Say that to yourself...stop! Come on and say it with me.
13   One...two...three...stop! Sometimes you have to turn off the
14   noise in your head. Now take a deep breath. Come on, do it
15   with me. *(Takes a deep breath.)* And another one. *(Inhales and*
16   *exhales.)* Now take another breath and let the air go out slowly.
17   It's sorta like letting the air out of a balloon before it pops.

18   Now what's got you wired? If you have too much to do,
19   forget about doing everything and make a list of two or three
20   things or maybe even one important thing you can do today.
21   One thing. Give yourself a little pep talk and do it! "OK,
22   Leroy/Lucy, get out there and mow that lawn. If you start now
23   you can finish in an hour...one hour and then you can play ball
24   like you wanted to in the first place." If you got a lot of stuff,
25   make a list of what's most important and check 'em off as you
26   finish.

27   If you're mad and uptight at someone, write a letter. You
28   don't have to mail anything. Write it and say everything you
29   want to say. *(Pantomimes writing.)* Oh, yes! What language!
30   What fun! Write it down, get it out. *(Pantomimes wadding up*
31   *the paper.)* Then throw it away. *(Big sigh)* What a relief just to
32   get it out. Then you can have a talk if you need to.

33   Maybe you're not the letter-writing kind. Have a little talk
34   with the person you're mad at, but practice first. Let me
35   demonstrate. Pull up another chair. *(Pantomimes pulling up*

1   *chair.*) You sit in one and imagine the other person is sitting
2   across from you. OK, here goes.
3   "Ah, Joey/Jennifer, when you told everybody at lunch I
4   liked Marty/Melissa, I felt like an idiot, and I wanted to beat
5   your face in. What I told you was between you and me. I
6   thought I could trust you. I'm mad at you. I know
7   Marty/Melissa doesn't like me or he/she wouldn't have
8   ignored me after you said that, and everybody at school was
9   ragging on me about it for the rest of the day. Right now I
10   really *hate* you!"
11   Well, you get the idea, the important thing is to say what
12   you're thinking and feeling. It helps just to hear yourself, then
13   you can decide what to do.
14   Of course, when all else fails, call a friend, or maybe you
15   have an older brother or sister you can talk to. And don't
16   forget your parents. Yeah, your parents. Believe it or not, they
17   were kids once. I like to talk to my friend's mom. She's a good
18   listener.
19   There are other things you can do, like relaxing, getting
20   your mind on something else. Just taking time to think things
21   out before you act. *Chill out.*
22   OK...one more time now. Close your eyes. (*Demonstrates.*)
23   Take a deep breath and be a cloud floating... (*He/she continues*
24   *as curtain closes.*)
25
26
27
28
29
30
31
32
33
34
35

55. On a Mountaintop

1   This is my secret place, here on this mountaintop. I used
2   to pretend I was an explorer, a mountain climber charting
3   unknown territory, climbing higher than anyone else. That's
4   my house down there. Actually, it's my grandpa's house...
5   Grampy. When he got sick, we came here to live with him. We
6   tried to get him to move to town and live with us, but Grampy
7   said ol' Shep would never take to city ways. Shep is Grampy's
8   dog, and in dog years, I guess he's about as old as my grandpa.
9   Anyway, my dad and mom, Jessie, my sister, and I moved up
10 there two years ago to take care of Grampy. Actually, I don't
11 think he really needed taking care of, but my dad worried a
12 lot.
13 *(Breathes deeply.)* I like it here. *(Stands, pointing left.)*
14 There's a trail that leads around a waterfall, and the river
15 runs down the mountain into Lake Toxaway, but the water is
16 so cold it'll make your lips blue even in the summertime. The
17 sun comes up right over those ridges and at night you can see
18 the lights of three towns twinkle *(Points)* there and there and
19 there, if there isn't fog. On a clear day, you can see Chimney
20 Rock way above the rest.
21 Grampy says the earth is in trouble. All those trees over
22 there on Tucker's Ridge and those down in the gap are dying.
23 See that dead wood? Some kind of insect lays eggs in the bark
24 and larva that causes damage, but the biggest problem is acid
25 rain – the pollution all around – cars, trucks and factories.
26 They used to do some mining around here, too. Stuff gets into
27 the water from the old mine shafts. Grampy says when he first
28 came up here there were a lot more squirrels and rabbits, big
29 herds of deer, and even a family of bears that lived over in
30 those caves near the river... *(Long pause)* But not now.
31 In this spot I've seen a few doe and some fawns, and
32 every once in awhile a big ol' buck comes by. One has a rack

1   this big. *(Arms extended.)* **Grampy talks about Ol' One Eye —**
2   **biggest deer he ever saw in these parts. Used to hunt him with**
3   **his rifle, but after so many years, Grampy said Ol' One Eye was**
4   **a relic from the past and deserved to be left alone.**
5   This place is magic. When I come up here, no matter how
6   bad I'm feeling, I get better. When I sit down on this spot right
7   here and take off my shoes and dig my toes down in the dirt, I
8   feel like one of these big ol' trees with roots going deep down
9   into the earth. And I think about the rocks...whole families of
10 stone, and I feel better. Some things don't change much if
11 they're not bothered. And what seems to matter so much
12 down there doesn't matter at all up here.
13   I'm afraid that someday I'll have to leave this place or
14 maybe something will happen to change things. My grampy
15 says you can't worry about what might happen 'cause that
16 spoils what's good right now.
17   *(Slower)* So, I guess I'll just dig my toes in a little deeper
18 and watch the sun go down behind those trees and figure it's
19 gonna come back up again tomorrow. *(Pause)* That's the way
20 it's always been. *(Slower. Long pause)* **Maybe somebody**
21 **somewhere is taking care of everything.** *(Looks up.)* **I hope so.**
22
23
24
25
26
27
28
29
30
31
32
33
34
35

ABOUT THE AUTHOR

© Eleanor Koets

Stephanie Fairbanks is a teacher and consultant with a M.A. degree in gifted education. She has been an adjunct instructor for Florida State University and the University of West Florida. She also coordinated the governor's summer program for gifted middle school students at the University of South Florida.

Stephanie has been involved in theatre as an actor, director and playwright. She began writing monologs as part of the writing and acting workshops she designed for her students. Her scripts have been used in the classroom, for auditions, and in competition.

Stephanie and her husband Greg Smallwood live with Carthage, their cat, in Summerville, South Carolina.